How To Boss Your Fonts Around

second edition

A primer on
font technology and
font management
on the Macintosh

Robin Williams

Peachpit Press ■ Berkeley ■ California

Acknowledgments

*Many thanks to **Roger Levit** of Santa Rosa, California, **Jim Alley** of Savannah, Georgia, and **Doug Miles** of Ellensburg, Washington, for taking the time to tech-edit this book. And to **Matt Deathrage** for kindly correcting my errors in the first edition, thus making the second edition better.*

*And I thank **Nancy Davis, Kate Reber,** and **Jenifer Blakemore** for helping to prevent me from embarrassing myself.*

❤

This book is fondly, warmly,
with love and a smile,
dedicated to my little sister,
Shannon Williams,
who calls font technology
"The F word."

How to Boss Your Fonts Around second edition
Robin Williams

©1998 Robin Williams

Peachpit Press
1249 Eighth Street
Berkeley, California 94710
800.283.9444
510.524.2178
510.524.2221 FAX

Find us on the World Wide Web at http://www.peachpit.com
Peachpit Press is a division of Addison Wesley Longman

ISBN 0-201-69640-1
0 9 8 7 6 5 4 3 2 1

Printed and bound in the United States of America

Contents

contents

Part II *Installing Fonts* 43

Part III 51
Font Management

The Purpose

This purpose of this little book is to give you power. Have you ever had a power struggle with your fonts? Well, if you actually **read** this book I guarantee **you** will be in total control. Never again will font names disappear from your menu, the wrong font show up on your screen, or a font transmogrify in the printer into the dreaded Courier. Your fonts will behave just as you expect, and if perchance they kick up a fuss, you will have the power to put them back in their place.

What this book does *not* discuss is which typeface to use in your work; there is no discussion of designing with type or of creating fine typography. An interesting thing these days is that everyone, prima donna designers included, not only has to know how to use type aesthetically, but also how to control the technology. This book discusses the technology; for the aesthetics of type, read *The Mac is not a typewriter, The Non-Designer's Design Book, The Non-Designer's Type Book,* and, for web type stuff, *The Non-Designer's Web Book.*

I strongly suggest you start at the beginning of this book, rather than in the middle of the font management section. I know, I know, you don't wanna start at the beginning, but there are so many terms in this book and you really have to understand exactly what I am referring to if you want control. If you jump in the middle, you might get yourself confused and then you'd blame me. Even if you think you know everything, at least skim through the first section. It's not that bad.

Whenever you see a word in *italic,* it means that word is explained or defined some-where else in this book. If there is a page number mentioned, the explanation is on that page, of course. Otherwise, check the glossary, or check the index for a reference to where a more thorough explanation can be found.

Good luck, and *be the Boss!*

Robin

Quick Check

Which System are you running?

The "System" is the software that runs the computer. At the moment, your Macintosh may be "running" one of these Systems:

- **Mac OS 8**
- **System 7.1** and higher (such as **7.5, 7.5.5, 7.5.6**)
- **System 7.0** or 7.0.1
- **System 6** or earlier

Unfortunately, installing fonts is slightly different for each of these various System versions, so it is important that you know which one you are running.

This book covers only **Mac OS 8!** And if you are using **System 7.1** or higher, just about everything in this book will be the same as OS 8—the pictures on your screen will look a little different from the pictures in the book.

But if you are using System 7.0 or any version of System 6, you need to get the first edition of this book from Peachpit Press.

Check your Apple menu

To see which System you are running, go to the Apple menu and choose "About This Computer..." or "About this Macintosh..." (whichever one it says).

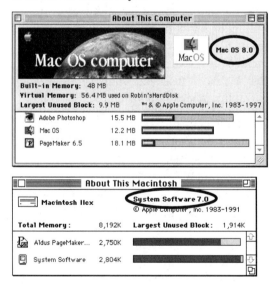

In the upper right of the dialog box is the version of System Software your Mac is running.

Part I

Font Technology

There are a lot of terms thrown around in the area of computer font technology, and before we go any further we need to clarify them. Knowing exactly what these terms refer to will give you control over your fonts, will help you understand why certain things happen and how to make other things happen. This section explains these terms:

PostScript vs. **QuickDraw**

Typeface, font, and **family**

Bitmapped font and **screen font**

Outline font and **printer font**

PostScript font and **Type 1 font**

Scalable font and **TrueType font**

Resident font and **downloadable font**

Adobe Type Manager (ATM) and
    Adobe Type Manager Deluxe

Printers: PostScript or QuickDraw

Why should you care?

All through this book I make references to *PostScript printers* and *non–PostScript printers* or *QuickDraw printers.* Your understanding of many aspects of font technology depends on understanding the difference between the two basic sorts of printers and knowing which kind you have.

PostScript printers

PostScript is a *page description language,* a powerful graphical programming language that describes how to create complex letterforms, such as *PostScript fonts*, and certain kinds of graphics, such as *EPS files*. You can open PostScript files in a word processor and read them. If you know how, you can edit the files to change things.

A *PostScript printer* has a *processor* (the chip that runs it) and *memory,* just like your computer; in fact, a PostScript printer is sometimes more powerful than the computer on your desk. The computer in the printer interprets the PostScript language that the pages are described with and tells the printer how to produce the pages. Because PostScript printers are actually computers, they tend to be rather expensive.

Even if the typeface on your screen looks jaggy and bitmapped, a PostScript printer will interpret the PostScript file for that typeface and print it with smooth edges (well, it will do this for *PostScript fonts* as long as it can find the *printer font,* but we'll talk about that later).

You might have a PostScript laser printer in your home or office. *Service bureaus* have much more expensive PostScript printers (like $100,000 expensive), and they can print your files in much higher *resolution* (which basically means higher quality), but the process is the same.

Now, the resolution of PostScript printers is an interesting thing: Your personal laser printer may have a resolution of 600 *dots per inch,* and the *imagesetter* (printer) at your service bureau may have a resolution of 2,540 dots per inch. A page that you create on your computer will go through any PostScript printer and come out with *whatever resolution that printer produces.* The same page will print at 600 dots per inch on your printer at home and at 2,540 dots per inch on an imagesetter.

PostScript-compatible printers

You will also hear of "PostScript-compatible" printers, which are printers that aren't *really* PostScript, but they can fake it pretty well. They don't contain a true PostScript interpreter, but they do have another interpreter that can do the job.

There is divided opinion about PostScript-compatible printers—some people feel that if you are going to be doing serious graphic design you should spend the money on true PostScript rather than try to fake it; others feel that a good PostScript-compatible printer can be a wonderful workhorse even for major projects such as newspapers and magazines. I hold the first opinion, but there are many people who are happy with their PostScript clones.

All through this book, whenever I refer to a "PostScript" printer, I mean PostScript or compatible.

Non-PostScript printers (QuickDraw)

A non-PostScript printer cannot interpret the PostScript language, but can only reproduce what it sees on the screen. The icons, text, windows, graphics, etc., that you see on the Macintosh screen are displayed using the *QuickDraw* language, a programming language developed by Apple. Printers that print just what is on the screen are often called *QuickDraw printers,* although there is really nothing QuickDraw in the printer itself—the printer doesn't even know Quick-Draw exists.

If the typeface on your screen looks jaggy and bitmapped, a non-PostScript printer will print it jaggy and bitmapped.

How do you know if your printer is PostScript or QuickDraw?

If your printer was really cheap, like less than $500, it's not PostScript or even Post-Script compatible. Other than that clue, you usually have to ask someone who **knows** those things (implying that some salespeople in consumer stores don't really know). Often the owner's guide or manual doesn't even come right out and tell you.

These printers are definitely **not** PostScript: HP LaserJet, DeskWriter, or DeskJet; Apple StyleWriter, LaserWriter sc, Personal Laser-Writer, and Personal LaserWriter ls, or any color ink jet printer. (HP has a PostScript cartridge for some of its DeskWriters.)

Typeface, family, and font

Some people are constantly trying to educate the masses (that's us) on the traditional difference between the terms **typeface** and **font** because they are actually not the same thing, much as we use the two terms interchangeably. So what follows is the distinction, and you can just store this information somewhere in the back of your brain.

Typeface
The **typeface** is the designed look of the characters, the structure of the letterforms. A designer designs a typeface.

Family
A **family** is a collection of all the sizes and styles of a type design with the same name and characteristics. For instance, "Times" is the name of a family. There is Times Regular, Times Italic, Times Bold, Times Bold Italic, perhaps Times Condensed, etc. They may have different styles, such as italic or bold, but they maintain their similar characteristics.

Simple and complex families
You'll hear references to "simple" families and "complex" families, and the distinction is often important when it comes time to organize your fonts, or when you run into a *merged* family (we'll talk about *merged* families later).

A **simple family** is one with only the four standard members: Regular, Italic, Bold, and Bold Italic (or it may, of course, have less). If a simple family has been *merged* (usually by the font vendor) you will see only the main family name in your menu, and you can use keyboard shortcuts or menu commands to set the Italic, Bold, and Bold Italic.

A **complex family** has additional typeface members, such as Black, Condensed, Ultra, Extended, Swash, and others. Even if a complex family has been *merged,* you will see the extra members' names in the menu. You must choose the actual typeface from the menu; there are no keyboard shortcuts to select the additional complex members.

Simple family	Complex family
Times Regular	Franklin Gothic Book
Times Italic	*Franklin Gothic Oblique*
Times Bold	**Franklin Gothic Bold**
Times Bold Italic	***Franklin Gothic Bold Oblique***
	Franklin Gothic No. 2
	Franklin Gothic Heavy
	Franklin Gothic Condensed
	Franklin Gothic Extra Condensed

Font

Traditionally, a **font** is one typeface in *one size and one style and one weight.* For example, Times Regular 10 point used to be one font; Times Regular 12 point was another font; Times Bold 12 point was another font; Times Bold Italic 12 point was another font. This stems from the days when type was made out of metal and each separate font had to be cut or ordered from a supplier and each font was kept in its own case: there was a box for the Times Regular 10 point and another box for the Times Regular 12 point and another for the Times Bold 12 point, etc.

But as you well know, we don't use our type that way anymore. At this point in history we can't possibly call each separate point size a separate font. And the menus are all labeled "Font" with the list of typeface names, so millions of people are being educated that the list of typeface names is a list of fonts. Our language changes, and some may say it is safe to assume that the term *font* has come to mean the same as *typeface* and we just have to accept it.

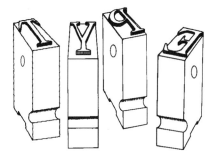

But this one distinction is important: ***each member of a typeface family is a separate font.*** That is, Times Regular is one font; Times Italic is another font; Times Bold is another font; Times Bold Italic is another font. Each individual member of a family had to be redesigned by the designer, and each one has individual files representing it.

- *Aesthetically, what we see displayed on the screen or printed onto paper is the* **typeface.** *The computer itself considers the internal source of its information to be the* **font.**

Bitmapped fonts and screen fonts

A **bitmapped font** is a font that is created by sending tiny electronic *bits* of information to certain pixels, or dots, on the screen and those bits turn the pixels on or off (black or white). That on/off information (the *bit*) is *mapped* to the grid of pixels on the screen. That's why bitmapped fonts are also known as **screen fonts**—they are bitmapped so they can be displayed on the *screen*.

 *The little squares you see represent an example of how the pixels may display a letter S on the screen. Each dot represents one pixel; each pixel is turned on by one bit of information.*

You may have seen type on your screen such as that shown below and wondered why your type was looking "bitmapped."

Bitmapped font

Well, every character you see on the screen, whether it looks jaggy or smooth, is actually bitmapped, because *there is no other way for the computer to display type on your screen*. The only reason some type does

not look so jaggy is because of the various technologies that improve the bitmapped shape (ATM and *TrueType,* for instance, which are both explained later).

You see, when the Mac was first developed there was nothing except screen fonts. These bitmapped screen fonts were designed around the *resolution* of the Mac screen, which was 72 pixels per inch, and the only printer at the time, the ImageWriter, had a similar resolution. So the characters in the typefaces were designed so they could be readable at that chunky resolution (be sure you read the next section on "Installed sizes").

Then the *PostScript* technology was created, and fonts had an added dimension—the *printer font* (info on this in a few pages). With PostScript fonts, there is a screen font that appears on the screen (and whose name appears in your menu), and a corresponding printer font that goes to the printer, and you have to have both parts of the font to print it. So you will often hear people talk about the screen font as opposed to the printer font.

It's important that you also read Chapter 4 on "City-named fonts." *(Ha—you're gonna end up reading the whole book!)*

Installed sizes

Bitmapped fonts (screen fonts) of any name are also called **fixed-size fonts.** They will appear somewhat smoother on your screen when you use a size that has been installed in the System. How do you know which sizes have been installed? One way is to click your mouse inside some text and then look at your Size menu. Most programs (except Microsoft Word) show the installed sizes in an outline style number, like this: 12.

Size
Other...
6
8
9
✓ 10
11
12
14
18
24
30
36
48
60

The sizes displayed in an outline style indicate that those particular sizes have been installed in the System. In this list, you can see that 10 and 12 point of the selected font have been installed.

*If **every** size is outlined, the selected text is TrueType, which is explained on pages 37–40.*

When you choose one of these installed sizes, the computer knows just how to map it to the screen. When you choose another size, though, the computer has to figure out how to create that size and it just can't do a very good job faking it. You can see below that 12 point Boston, which is installed, looks cleaner than the 13 point, which is not installed (that's why screen fonts are also called **fixed-size fonts**).

Boston font
Boston font

Another way to see what sizes of screen fonts are installed is to look in the folder where they are stored.

What screen font icons look like

In any version of System 7 or OS 8, this is what screen fonts look like in the folder:

Screen fonts are often stored in suitcase icons (this icon has nothing to do with the Suitcase program!!!). Double-click on a suitcase to open its window.

FranklinGothic

If you view your suitcase window as Icons, this is what screen fonts look like.

FranklinGothic 12

FranklinGothic (bold) 12

If you view by Name or List, you will see these.

🅰 FranklinGothic (bold) 12
🅰 FranklinGothic (italic) 12
🅰 FranklinGothic 12

Sometimes in a list the name is too long and you can't see its size. In OS 8, click once on the file name and it will condense to fit the entire name. In System 7, view the window by Icon and the full name of the screen font and its size will be visible.

🅰 C FranklinGothic Condensed 12
🅰 EC FranklinGothic ExtraCond 12

You can always install more screen sizes (fixed sizes) of your fonts if you have them available (see Chapter 10 on installing fonts). But before you run off and install a bunch more sizes, read on about *outline fonts,* ATM, and *TrueType.*

City-named fonts

Most **city-named fonts,** such as Boston, San Francisco, Cairo, New York, or Geneva, are *bitmapped, fixed-size, screen fonts,* and that's all there is to them. They were designed for the low *resolution* of the Macintosh screen and for the original Apple printer, the ImageWriter; that is, they were designed within the limitations of those relatively large dots.

(If you are using OS 8 or System 7, your city-named fonts Chicago, Geneva, New York, and Monaco are *TrueType,* another font technology which we'll discuss in a minute. TrueType fonts, whether named after a city or not, will look smooth on the screen and will print nicely to any printer. But everything else in this section applies to any font with a city name. It's important to be aware of when you are using a city-named font, and learn when you should use them and when you should avoid them.)

If you use a city-named font, such as Cairo or New York, in an *installed size* (see the previous page), the type will be quite legible on the screen and when printed to an old printer like an ImageWriter. The text will actually be more legible than if you use a non–city-named font, because a non–city-named font, such as Palatino, was designed in a completely different way and has to scrunch itself to fit into the dots on the screen. Notice below that New York 12-point on the screen is actually clearer than Palatino 12-point, even though 12-point Palatino is also installed.

New York   12 point
Palatino   12 point

Printing to a non-PostScript printer

When you print to a *non-PostScript printer* (such as the HP DeskJet or DeskWriter, color ink jet printers, or an Apple StyleWriter), the printer will print what appears on the screen. That is, if the type looks jagged and clunky on the screen, it will print jagged and clunky. If it looks fairly smooth, it will print fairly smooth. This is true regardless of the typeface name.

Printing non–city-named fonts to a PostScript printer

If you print a *non*–city-named font to a *Post-Script printer,* the font, no matter how awful it looks on the screen, will usually print just beautifully.

Palatino 12 point, on the screen
Palatino 12 point, printed

Printing city-named fonts to a PostScript printer

If you print to a PostScript printer, a *city-named* font will print close to how you see it on the screen—if it looks dorky, it's gonna print dorky. But a PostScript printer really doesn't like city-named fonts; it doesn't know what to do with them. Three fonts in particular can cause problems: New York, Geneva, and Monaco. Some programs, such as Microsoft Word, know the printer doesn't like fonts such as New York, Geneva, and Monaco, and so it has a default to automatically substitute fonts. When this happens, Times is substituted for New York, Helvetica is substituted for Geneva, and Courier is substituted for Monaco. But remember, these non–city-named fonts are designed for high-resolution, and so they don't fit in the same space as the low resolution city-named fonts. The substitution causes awkward space between the words, indents don't line up, and underlines are dashed.

> This is a city-named font, New York,
> that was automatically
> substituted with Times.
> Notice the terrible word spacing
> and the dashes _____ in this line.

(**TrueType city-named fonts,** except for those three—New York, Geneva, and Monaco—will generally print fine to a PostScript printer; see the chapter on TrueType.)

Don't print city-named fonts to an imagesetter (at a service bureau)

If you print city-named fonts to a PostScript *imagesetter* (all imagesetters are PostScript) you will really have problems. The image-setter doesn't just dislike city-named fonts, it freaks out and often simply refuses to print. If you're lucky, every city-named font will turn into Courier instead of stopping the machine.

```
This is Courier. Were you ever
    surprised to see this
        on your page?
```

City-named fonts with ATM

Fonts that ***do not have*** a city name will appear smooth on the screen and will print even smoother to any printer when you use *ATM* (*Adobe Type Manager;* pages 31–36), no matter what size is installed. The example below shows an actual screen shot of a typeface on my screen at 15.5 point.

Shelley Volante on the screen

But city-named fonts (other than TrueType), will never appear as smooth, as you can see in the example below, an actual screen shot of Boston at 18 point, installed. To find out why, read about *printer fonts.*

Boston font

When to use city-named fonts

Keep city-named fonts where they belong—on your screen and on your non-PostScript printer. If you are working in a database, spreadsheet, or word processor and you want to type fast and be able to read the screen clearly, use a city-named font in an installed size. If you want web pages to be easy to read, change your browser default to a city-named font. *But before you print to a PostScript printer, change the text or the browser default to a non–city-named font!*

PostScript fonts

PostScript fonts are fonts that use the Adobe *PostScript* technology. In addition to the *bitmapped, screen* information that displays the typeface on the screen (which you just read about on pages 16–17), a PostScript font contains information for a *PostScript printer,* information that has been written in the *PostScript language.* This printer information tells the printer how to create that typeface on the page with nice, smooth edges.

Because PostScript fonts have these two separate pieces of information, one for the screen and one for the printer, they are actually divided into two separate files called the *screen font* and the *printer font.* All PostScript fonts have these two separate parts, and these two parts must be stored together in pairs.

Outline fonts
The two parts of PostScript fonts are the screen font and the printer font. The printer font contains mathematical **outlines** of each of the characters. Because these outlines are mathematical instead of *bitmapped,* the computer can use the math formulas and *scale* the outlines—the formulas—to any

size you like (that's why outline fonts are also called **scalable fonts).**

This is the actual outline of the letter R in the font Garamond Light. Because it is a math formula that defines the outline, the letter can be scaled (enlarged or reduced) to any size.

You must have a matched pair—**both** the bitmapped, screen portion of the font **and** the printer portion—if you want to print a PostScript outline font. When you buy an outline font, you will find both of those parts on the disk. The screen font family usually resides in a *suitcase* icon (see the following page). The printer fonts are separate files, separate icons, one icon for each member of the family that is stored inside the suitcase. I'll explain this in detail several more times.

 + =

This is the bitmapped letter you see on the screen.   *This outline of the letter is sent to the printer.*   *This is the result on the printed page.*

*Each PostScript font has two parts: the **bitmapped, screen font** and the **outline, printer font**.*

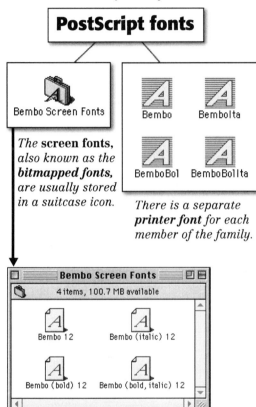

*The **screen fonts,** also known as the **bitmapped fonts,** are usually stored in a suitcase icon.*

*There is a separate **printer font** for each member of the family.*

Notice there is a printer font (above right) that matches each screen font in this suitcase. If there is not a matched pair of bitmap font and printer font, the font will not print correctly!

Scalable fonts

If a font is *scalable,* it means the characters can be "scaled" (enlarged or reduced) to any size and printed without any distortion or jaggy edges, whether that screen size has been installed in the System or not.

Both PostScript fonts and *TrueType fonts* are scalable. TrueType fonts are automatically scaled on the screen and to any kind of printer (which simply means they look smooth on the screen and on the printed page). PostScript fonts are only scaled **automatically** to *PostScript printers;* if you would like them scaled to the screen and to *non-PostScript printers,* you need to invest in *Adobe Type Manager (ATM).*

Without Adobe Type Manager (details on pages 31–36), a PostScript font will look chunky and jaggy on the screen (as shown below). When you print that typeface to a PostScript printer, though, it will print just beautifully (as shown in the second example below). **But** if you print a chunky and jaggy PostScript font to a *non*-PostScript printer, it will look just as bad on paper as it does on the screen—the non-PostScript printer cannot use the outline to scale the font but must get all its information from the bitmapped screen font.

This is a Type 1, outline, scalable font on the screen without ATM.

This is exactly the same scalable font
as shown directly above,
printed to a PostScript printer.

PostScript Types

Type 1 fonts

A *Type 1 font* is always a PostScript font. Type 1 used to be a proprietary format (that means Adobe owned it and didn't want to share), but now the specifications are public and anyone can create Type 1 fonts.

Type 2 fonts

There are no *Type 2 fonts*. There was once a font technology proposed as Type 2, but it didn't make it past the drawing board.

Type 3 fonts

Before Adobe made the specifications public for creating Type 1 fonts, everyone else had to create *Type 3 fonts*. Type 3 fonts are also PostScript. They have larger file sizes, are slower to print, and don't print as well at small sizes, but they can have shades and decorations inside the letterforms. There are not many Type 3 fonts around now; most have been converted to Type 1.

ATM does not work on Type 3 fonts. Some versions of System 7 will not print Type 3 fonts. ATM Deluxe reports a Type 3 font as damaged and will not open it, but in OS 8 you can install a Type 3 font pair directly into your Fonts folder in the System Folder and it will print just fine. It won't look very good on the screen, but it will print.

You can usually tell a Type 3 font by its printer icon—it often has a number "3" in it somewhere. Type 1 fonts often (but not always) have the number "1" in the icon.

- *All PostScript fonts are Type 1; all Type 1 fonts are PostScript.*
- *Outline fonts can be Type 1, Type 3, or TrueType.*
- *All outline fonts are scalable; all scalable fonts are outline.*
- *TrueType fonts are not PostScript.*

- *The terms "bitmapped font," "screen font," and "fixed-size font" all refer to the same thing—a font that has been created to be displayed on the screen.*

Fonts on the Web

Surf the Web with city-named fonts

Because city-named fonts were designed for low resolution screen display, they are your best choice to use as the default font in your web browser. Take a look at the examples below to see how much easier it is to read a city-named font on a web page (especially when it's on your screen and not in print, as it is here). Change the default font in your browser through the Options or Preferences settings, as shown below.

Print non–city-named fonts

When you *print* a web page, however, you don't want to print city-named fonts! So before you print, change your browser's default to Times or Helvetica (or Garamond or Syntax or any other font you prefer).

Specify city-named fonts

If you create web pages and specify certain fonts to appear, please specify Geneva before Helvetica and New York before Times. The page will look cleaner and the visitor will be able to read the text easier.

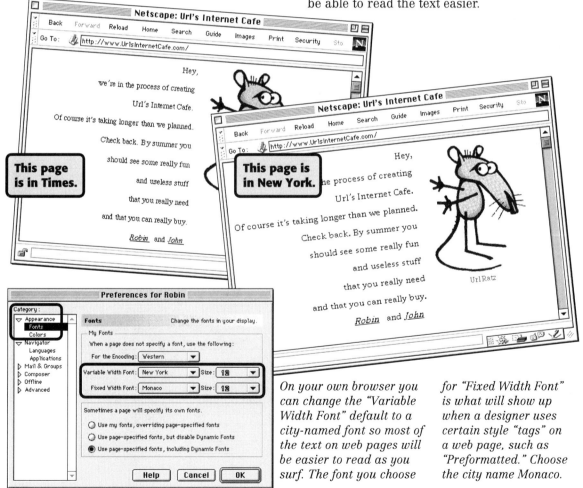

On your own browser you can change the "Variable Width Font" default to a city-named font so most of the text on web pages will be easier to read as you surf. The font you choose

for "Fixed Width Font" is what will show up when a designer uses certain style "tags" on a web page, such as "Preformatted." Choose the city name Monaco.

Screen and printer fonts

These two pages elaborate on the screen and printer fonts that comprise all PostScript fonts (you read the previous four pages, right?). The screen font information presented here is applicable to any *bitmapped, screen font*, as well as to *TrueType*.

Screen fonts

Screen fonts are usually stored in a suitcase icon *(figure 1)*. Although you can store screen fonts elsewhere, it is impossible to put anything except screen fonts and *TrueType* into a suitcase.

Don't get these cute little suitcase icons confused with the font management program called *Suitcase!* They have nothing to do with each other!

In OS 8 or any version of System 7, when you double-click on a suitcase icon it opens into a window, just like any folder *(figure 2)*.

Each of the icons inside the suitcase represents one size of screen font *(figure 3)*.

If you double-click on the name of a font, another little window will open and display the font in that size *(figure 4)*.

Why do you need screen fonts?

Bottom line: if you don't have a screen font installed, you won't see the font in the menu! Also, the screen font holds the *font metrics* for a typeface.

Index.bmap

❶ *Some suitcases may be labeled with ".bmap" or ".scr" or some other indication to remind you this is the bitmapped, screen font.*

❷ *If you double-click on a suitcase in OS 8 or in any version of System 7, you see a folder storing icons that represent the screen fonts in each of their sizes. These are the sizes you can install in your System.*

suitcase window viewed by Icon   *suitcase window viewed by Name*

❸ *Each of these files is a screen font. The number in its name is the size of the font.*

Index-Book 12   Index-Book 24

❹ *If you double-click on one of the font sizes, you will see a sample of the font in that size.*

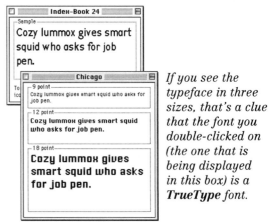

If you see the typeface in three sizes, that's a clue that the font you double-clicked on (the one that is being displayed in this box) is a **TrueType** *font.*

Printer fonts

I'm assuming you read the information on the previous pages that explains what the printer font is and does. Different font vendors have different printer font icons, as shown below (*figure 5*).

You should have one printer font to match each screen font family member, as shown in figures 6 and 7.

If you double-click on a printer font icon, you will get a message telling you that the computer uses this file (*figure 8*). You can't actually *look* at anything except the icon.

Remember, printer fonts provide information to the PostScript printer, not to you.

❺ *These examples show printer fonts from different vendors.*

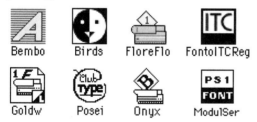

Bembo Birds FloreFlo FontoITCReg

Goldw Posei Onyx ModulSer

Never change the name of a printer font!

❻ *Below on the left is the closed Garamond suitcase. On the right is the open suitcase. Notice there are four members to this family: Garamond Book, Book Italic, Bold, and Bold Italic. In many suitcases you will find more than one fixed-size bitmap for each family member. If you use Adobe Type Manager, you only need to keep one bitmap size for each individual font.*

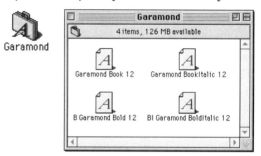

Garamond

Garamond
4 items, 126 MB available

Garamond Book 12   Garamond BookItalic 12

B Garamond Bold 12   BI Garamond BoldItalic 12

❼ *For each of the family members shown above, you must have a separate printer font, as shown below. That's because Garamond Book has a different design and thus different outlines from Garamond Book Italic; they are actually different, individual fonts in the same family.*

GaramBoo   GaramBoolta   GaramBol   GaramBolIta

❽ *The printer font icon represents data that is sent to the printer. There is nothing for you to look at or do anything with.*

PostScript™ font
This is a file that your computer uses to display characters. To use this font, place this file in the Fonts folder.

OK

Resident and downloadable fonts

Resident fonts

Resident fonts are *Type 1 PostScript fonts* whose *printer font* information lives inside the *PostScript laser printer.*

You see, a PostScript printer has a CPU (central processing unit, the tiny chip that runs the machine) inside of it just like your computer. A PostScript printer *is* a computer. The printer also has *memory* (RAM) built into it, which is where your pages and odd fonts temporarily hang out while you print. Whatever hangs around in memory automatically disappears when the printer is turned off.

A PostScript printer also has ROM (read-only memory). The information built into the ROM chips is permanent; it does not disappear when you turn off the printer. *You* cannot put anything into ROM—whatever is there was programmed into it at the factory. ***The printer fonts for a number of different typefaces are programmed into the ROMs in PostScript printers.***

[In the list of resident PostScript printer fonts in the next column, notice there are no *city-named fonts*, such as Geneva or New York! Remember, city-named fonts that are not TrueType are composed **only** of bitmapped, screen information. They have no corresponding printer font that would live in ROM.]

For instance, in most Apple LaserWriters the printer fonts for the following typefaces live right in the ROMs, which is why you've never seen printer font icons for most of them:

Avant Garde, *Italic,* **Bold,** ***Bold Italic***

Bookman, *Italic,* **Bold,** ***Bold Italic***

Courier, *Italic,* **Bold,**
   Bold Italic

Helvetica, *Italic,* **Bold,** ***Bold Italic***

Helvetica Narrow, *Italic,* **Bold,** ***Bold Italic***

New Century Schoolbook, *Italic,*
   Bold, ***Bold Italic***

Palatino, *Italic,* **Bold,** ***Bold Italic***

Symbol: Ιλοϖεφοηντολλεττ

Times, *Italic,* **Bold,** ***Bold Italic***

Zapf Chancery

Zapf Dingbats: ✳❑✴■✳▲✿✳▼◆✳

When you print a page with any of the above-named fonts, the printer gets the *outline* data from its printer font that lives right inside the printer, and thus it merrily prints the face. These fonts whose outlines are stored in the printer's ROM are called **resident fonts.** You might also hear them called the "LaserWriter ROM fonts" or the "LaserWriter 35" (there are 35 separate fonts once you count the bolds and italics, etc.). Use a font downloader utility (page 30) to find out which fonts are resident in your PostScript printer.

(PostScript *imagesetters,* the high-resolution printers at the *service bureau,* do not have any resident fonts.)

Downloadable fonts

When you buy a PostScript font, you get a disk that contains a matched pair of the two separate parts: the *screen font* and the *printer font*. This outline, or printer font, obviously, is **not resident** in your printer; it was not programmed into the ROM (the read-only memory). Any font you buy (or acquire), then, is called a **downloadable font** because its printer font information must be *loaded down* into the printer before the type can be created on the page.

The printer font for downloadable fonts gets loaded, or stored, into the printer's RAM, (*random-access memory,* which is tempo-rary), not into its ROM (*read-only memory,* which was permanently programmed at the factory). Anything stored in RAM is "volatile," meaning it disappears when the power is turned off, so those downloadable printer fonts have to be downloaded again next time you turn on the printer and print.

Your PostScript printer has a limited amount of RAM. Whether you have one megabyte of RAM in your printer, or seven or more, it is possible to fill it up with too many printer fonts. If you have a great number of fonts in one document, it may take a long time to print because the printer fonts must be downloaded, then removed to make room for others, over and over again. How this process works depends on the application you are using and what you have chosen in the Page Setup and Print dialog boxes.

Any application will go through some sort of *automatic* downloading for you and you never have to think about it (except to make sure your printer fonts are in the correct location on your hard disk so the printer can find them). It is possible and appropriate in some jobs for you to *manually* download a number of printer fonts to speed up the printing. And if you have an astounding number of fonts available to you at all times, you may want to consider *permanently* downloading by means of a special hard disk. Details on each method of download-ing are found on the following pages.

Downloading the downloadables

If you read page 27, you know what **downloadable fonts** are (any outline font that did not come with your printer). These fonts have to be downloaded into the printer's *random-access memory* (RAM). *Resident fonts,* remember, are stored in the printer's ROM, which is permanent. But RAM is only a temporary storage place that is emptied whenever you turn off the power.

- *Font downloading is only necessary (or possible) when you print to a PostScript printer. QuickDraw, or non-PostScript, printers just print the TrueType or bitmapped screen fonts— so you can ignore this entire section if you use a non-PostScript printer.*

  For non-PostScript printers, ATM (Adobe Type Manager) or TrueType can significantly improve the look of the printed pages, as well as how the type looks on the screen.

Automatic downloading on PostScript printers

Font downloading can be handled ***automatically,*** which is probably what has been happening all this time unless you have consciously chosen another method. When you choose to print, the Mac automatically finds the *printer font* and downloads it into the printer's memory (RAM). If the memory gets full because you used a lot of fonts in your publication, the printer has to remove a font (flush it from memory) to make room for the new one.

Automatic downloading works quite well, particularly if your printer has at least two or three megabytes of RAM available and your publication doesn't use more than three or four fonts. (*Remember*, Goudy Regular is one printer font, Goudy Italic is another printer font, Goudy Bold is another printer font, etc., etc., etc.) However, if your printer has only 1 or 1.5 megs of RAM, then the printer has to keep flushing out one face and downloading another and it can get quite boring, as well as time-consuming.

Options for auto-downloading

Take a look at your Page Attributes or Page Setup dialog box: Depending on your software, you may find the "Options" button or "Post-Script Options" menu on your "Page Setup" dialog box from the File menu, as in Claris-Works, Microsoft Word, or QuarkXPress. In PageMaker, hold down the Option key as you choose "Print" from the File menu, then click "Setup" (in older versions, click "Options"). In some programs the Setup/Attributes dialog box will appear as the first or second message in the printing process. The dialog boxes look something like those shown at the bottom of this page, depending on your software versions.

If you check "Unlimited Downloadable Fonts," the printer will erase each font from memory before downloading the next one. But that means every time the printer comes across an italic word or a different typeface or a bold subhead, etc., the existing font is flushed from memory and the new one is loaded. This is *really* boring, but you must check this box if

you're using a lot of fonts and your printer doesn't have much RAM (less than two megs).

If you do **not** check "Unlimited Downloadable Fonts," (you probably haven't), the printer never erases fonts from memory. When the memory gets full—which it will if there are a large number of fonts, if your printer has only one meg of RAM, or if it's a long publication—the print job may just go belly-up. Of course, the more RAM you have, the less this is a problem, so if you have enough RAM (at least five or six megabytes) in your printer, make sure this button is **not** checked.

Should you manually download?

If you have not had trouble with automatic downloading and you don't find that it takes an interminable length of time, then you needn't worry about doing it any other way. You can stop reading this and go to lunch. If, however, you would like to speed up the process, you can *manually download* the printer fonts. Read on.

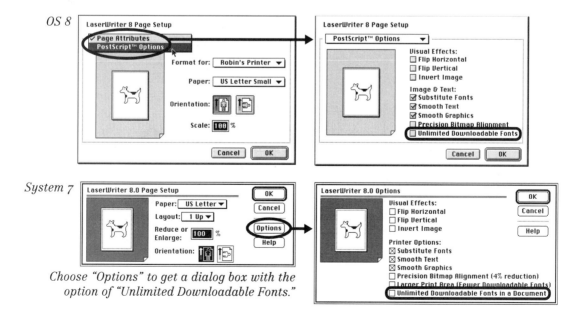

Choose "Options" to get a dialog box with the option of "Unlimited Downloadable Fonts."

Manual downloading

When you buy downloadable fonts, the font vendor almost always sends you a *font downloader utility* (if not, they are easy to find; search your computer for one you might have already, search online at www.shareware.com or www.download.com, or ask a friend). The icons from different vendors or different versions may look different:

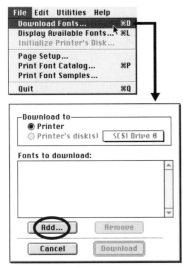

First turn on your printer and let it warm up, then double-click on the downloader icon. You will first get just a menu; from the File menu, choose "Download Fonts...."

Click the "Add..." button, then navigate to your fonts folder and select each font to download. Don't download too many fonts or you will fill up the available RAM and you won't be able to print at all!

If your printer memory is limited (which it probably is if you are having to manually download fonts), turn off the printer, then turn it back on again just before you download. This empties the RAM so you will have the maximum space available. (If other people are working on the same printer, warn them before you turn off the printer in the middle of their job.)

If the printer has only 1 or 1.5 megs of RAM, you can download only about three fonts (e.g., Goudy, Goudy Italic, Goudy Bold). You might be able to squeeze in a fourth (Goudy Bold Italic), but then you often won't have enough memory to print the publication. So rather than download every font in the publication, manually download just the font(s) your publication uses the most. As long as the printer font icons are in the proper place, the printer will be able to find and use the fonts that occur only occasionally.

Printer fonts that are manually downloaded are temporary. As soon as RAM is emptied (by turning off the printer, by a power failure, or by RAM getting too full—in which case the printer tells you to turn it off and on), everything stored in RAM disappears. So tomorrow, after the publication gets proofed and all the errors show up, you must download the fonts again when you come in to make corrections. After a few weeks of trying to print complex jobs you will be ready to add more RAM to your printer.

Permanent downloading

There is one permanent way of downloading fonts to your printer: buy a PostScript printer that allows you to connect a special hard disk that holds all your downloadable fonts. Once on that special hard disk, all your fonts will act like *resident fonts*.

Adobe Type Manager (ATM)

Adobe Type Manager (affectionately known as ATM) is a wonderful utility that no one should live without. It makes the type on your screen look almost as good as the laser-printed type on the page. This is an example of what it does for you:

This is what the letter Q (Shelley Volante font) looks like on the screen without ATM, even when the bitmap is installed.

Using ATM, this is what the same letter Q looks like on the same screen. Wow.

You don't have to do anything—you just install ATM and it does what it does automatically. On page 17 I mentioned that your *screen fonts* will display better if you use a size that is *installed* in your System, as indicated by the number in the outline style in the Size menu. Well, ATM makes every size of type look about as good on the screen as it will when printed to a *PostScript printer,* and even improves the look of installed bitmaps.

ATM only works with Type 1 fonts!

How ATM works

It's important to know how ATM does what it does, so when it doesn't work you'll have some clues as to how to fix it.

Let's begin with the PostScript printer. The *printer font* portion of a *Type 1 PostScript font* is just a bunch of data, or information. A *PostScript printer* can take that data, which describes the *outline* of each of the characters, and *rasterize* it. "Rasterize" means to convert the outlines into dots. Those outlines with the math formulas are each a series of straight, connected lines, but your laser printer prints in *dots per inch,* right? Your laser printer cannot print straight lines, it can only print dots. So the PostScript "interpreter" converts the straight lines to dots and tells the printing mechanism how to print that outline with dots and then fill it in.

Well, ATM uses the same rasterizing intelligence that the PostScript printer uses. ATM finds the printer font that matches the screen font you have chosen from your menu. It converts the outline data in the printer font into dots. Instead of sending these characters made of dots to the printer, though, ATM sends them to your screen.

But why . . . ?

Ah, you say, then what is on my screen is still nothing more than dots, or pixels. That sounds suspiciously just like a bitmapped, screen font. Why does it look so much better with ATM? The answer is that *ATM **simply does a better job**.* Screen fonts, as we discussed earlier, are known as "fixed-size" because they are designed for one point size, and that point size has been created within the limitation of the low resolution of a typical monitor. ATM creates the letter-form from the complex, *scalable outline* data, so it is not limited to a low-resolution fixed-size shape.

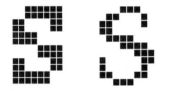

These letters have been radically enlarged so you can see the actual pixels that comprise each form. On the left is the fixed-size bitmap charac-ter; on the right is the same character rasterized by ATM. You can see that each letterform uses the same size of pixels and the same amount of space, but ATM chooses its pixels more carefully to create a better representation of the letter.

ATM vs. installed screen sizes

Several technically oriented people have told me that you actually get a better screen display with the installed *fixed-size bitmaps* than you do when ATM creates the screen type display. They say you should install more screen sizes for this reason. But look at these two screen shots that compare a

bitmapped screen font in an installed size without ATM, and the same font, same size that ATM put on the screen, using the outline. Which looks better to you?

> This is Times 10 point, installed , with
> ATM *not* working.

> This is Times 10 point, installed, with
> ATM working.

ATM with non-PostScript printers

If you have a *PostScript printer,* ATM's usefulness is just to make the type prettier on the screen ("just"—ha!). But ATM is particularly wonderful for those who do not have PostScript printers.

A *non-PostScript printer,* sometimes called a *QuickDraw printer* (see page 13), does not have a PostScript interpreter inside, nor does it have the rest of the computer parts necessary (like a CPU, RAM, or ROM) to *rasterize* PostScript fonts. But if ATM is installed on your Mac, ATM will do the PostScript interpretation right inside your computer—ATM will rasterize the outline data in the printer font **to the maximum resolution** of your printer. This means if you have a QuickDraw printer with a resolu-tion of 300 *dots per inch,* ATM will rasterize the font to 300 dots per inch. If your printer has a resolution of 400 dots per inch, ATM will rasterize the font to 400 dots per inch. In other words, if you use ATM you can print pages of text on your inexpensive printer that look as good as those from a PostScript printer. Yes, this is really as wonderful as it sounds.

ATM with resident fonts

Have you noticed that ATM doesn't work on some of the *resident fonts,* such as Palatino or Bookman?

This is Palatino on the screen, a resident font.

This is Bookman on the screen, also a resident font.

This is Bembo on the screen, a downloadable font.

ATM cannot *rasterize* resident fonts because, remember, their printer fonts live in the laser printer's ROM—those printer font files are not on your disk. So ATM ***can't find the printer fonts to rasterize them.*** If you use the resident fonts regularly and would like ATM to work on them, you can buy those printer fonts, called Adobe Type Basics, from Adobe Systems, Inc.

Is ATM already installed?

How can you tell if ATM is already installed and what version you have?

In Mac OS 8 or newer versions of System 7, look in the Control Panels folder inside the System Folder. Look for "~ATM."

In older versions of System 7, open the System Folder. View the window "By Name" and look for "~ATM." There may be other letters or numbers in the name, such as 68020/030 or ™.

Click once on the ATM file that you find in the Control Panels folder (as shown below, left), then press Command I to view the Get Info box (below, right). This box of information will tell you which version you have.

If you're running Mac OS 8, you need ATM version 3.9 at least. If you're running System 7.1, you need at least ATM version 3.0.

This is the file icon for ATM.

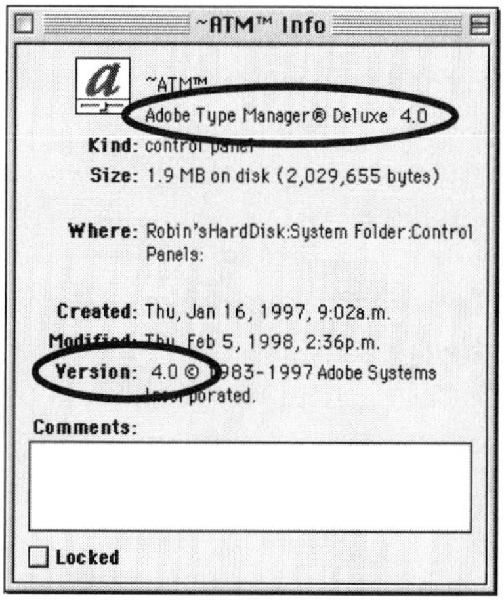

This is the Get Info box for Adobe Type Manager. It tells you the version number of the software.

33

ATM Deluxe vs. regular

What's the difference?

Very important! All through this book you will read about ATM and ATM Deluxe. The difference is very important. Until we get to the section on font management, I'm talking about the regular version of ATM that makes your type look great on the screen and on non-PostScript printers. ATM Deluxe also makes type look great, but **in addition** it has strong features for managing your fonts, allowing you to open just the ones you want when you want them.

The most important thing to know is this:

if you plan to use another font management utility such as Font Reserve, Suitcase, or MasterJuggler, you want to make sure you don't buy the *Deluxe* version of ATM. Now, a small problem is that you can't buy the non-deluxe version of ATM. At the time of this writing, Adobe is selling only the Deluxe edition (the Deluxe edition starts with version 4.0). Other versions of ATM, however, including the non-deluxe edition of version 4.0, are available on just about any Adobe CD. When you install Photoshop, PageMaker, Illustrator, or Acrobat, you usually get a non-deluxe version of ATM.

Read the "Read Me" file

Always read the Read Me files for any new software. Actually, you should print it and keep it with your manual. And you should read your manual, too.

ATM Deluxe 4.0 Read Me

There are important little tips about using Adobe Type Manager in the Read Me file.

The ATM control panel

ATM is a control panel and you can customize several of its features. Choose "~ATM™" from your Control Panels menu under the Apple menu. It's alphabetized at the end of the list.

This is the non-deluxe version of ATM 4.0:

In the Deluxe version of ATM, go to the File menu and choose "Preferences" to get this dialog box:

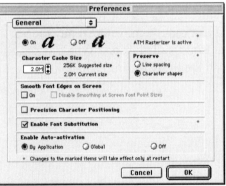

In versions of ATM before 4.0, this is what the control panel looks like.

On or Off

You can turn ATM **on** or **off,** obviously. You need to restart for this to take affect.

Character Cache Size or Font Cache

The **Cache** (pronounced "cash") shows the amount of system *memory* (RAM) ATM is grabbing to store the font data it creates. You can change this amount. Keep in mind that if ATM takes this RAM, no other applications on your computer can use it. If you don't have a lot of extra memory, don't allocate of a lot of it to ATM. How much should you allocate?

The **default** amount is 256K. Click the arrow keys to increase or decrease the amount.

Decrease cache: If you don't have a great many fonts in your document, you may want to *decrease* the amount of the font cache so you have more RAM available to run your other applications.

Leave cache as is: If you use SuperATM (see page 36) or a *multiple master* font, leave the cache at 256K, at least.

Increase cache: You may want to *increase* the amount of font cache if you find your characters disappearing or looking jagged (either on-screen or when printed); *or* if your application seems unusually slow when you turn pages, scroll, or when type is being drawn on the screen; *or* if you're using very large point sizes of type; *or* if you are using lots of fonts plus a multiple master or two.

Allow about 50K for each outline font you're using, and set the cache to the closest increment to that amount (the cache increases or decreases by set amounts). Don't set the cache beyond 512K for each 8 megs of RAM in your computer.

Preserve

The **Preserve line spacing** option is the default. This keeps the space between the lines the way you are used to. See the next option.

If you choose to **Preserve character shapes,** ATM will increase the bounding box (the space allowed for each character) around each letter so if you use capital letters with accent marks or other diacritical marks, the letters won't be squashed on the screen. But in some applications, like Word, this will change the line spacing.

If you use Photoshop and find that the tops or bottoms of letters are chopped off, choose to preserve the character shapes. In other applications, such as PageMaker or Quark-XPress, it doesn't matter if the letters appear chopped off on the screen because they will still print properly.

Smooth Font Edges on Screen

This option in versions 4.0 and above lets ATM "anti-alias" the edges of text so they appear smoother on the screen. To do this, ATM uses a variety of colors to soften the edges (see the example on page 74). Experiment with this option. On many web pages, it can make your type more difficult to read, depending on the colors ATM has available to anti-alias with.

If you notice "halos" around text or if the text appears too blurry, turn this option off.

Precision Character Positioning

This option enables ATM to position characters very precisely on the screen, even more so than previous versions of ATM. If you use Word or ClarisWorks, first turn on fractional widths before you choose this option: in Word, go to the Page Setup in the File menu; in ClarisWorks, turn it on in Preferences.

Enable Auto-activation

If you use a font management utility, you often open documents in which you've used fonts that aren't open at the moment. In the Deluxe version of ATM, you can choose to let ATM open any as-yet unloaded fonts that are in your document as you open the document. The fonts need to be in ATM's list of known fonts, so at first some fonts might not open until ATM learns where every single font you own resides.

Adobe PageMaker has its own font substitution feature, so you need to tell PageMaker to use ATM's feature. In the General Preferences, click the "Map fonts..." button. Click "ATM font matching."

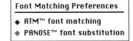

Now, if you do this in an open publication, *this feature will apply only to that publication.* To make ATM font matching a default for all future publications (ones not created yet), close all publication windows but leave PageMaker open. Go to the General Preferences and click the ATM font matching button.

Enable Font Substitution

In version 4.0 and above, the "font emulation" of *SuperATM* is built into ATM (see the following info). If you want any of your applications to create a substitute font in your documents for any typeface that is missing or just not loaded yet, check this box.

In some versions of ATM before 4.0, you will see an option to **Substitute for missing fonts.** If this option is dimmed (gray), it means the font database that SuperATM needs is missing. If you installed SuperATM properly, this option will be available. But you may see this gray item even if you don't have Super-ATM in your computer.

Font emulation

Have you ever opened a document, especially a document from someone else, and found the pages displaying the dreaded Courier because your Mac did not have the proper font? Certain versions of ATM, including an earlier version called SuperATM, prevent this problem by substituting a *multiple master font* for the font that is missing. The multiple master font emulates the *font metrics* of the missing typeface, so the lines of text end where they should, the weight of the substituted typeface looks similiar to the weight of the original face, and thus the layout of the document stays the same as it was originally intended. When the document goes back to a computer with the original font installed, the typeface turns back into what it was supposed to be in the first place. Font emulation is now built into all versions of ATM, and into Adobe Acrobat.

For font emulation/substitution to work, the ATM Font Database must be installed in the System Folder, and the multiple master font pairs called **Adobe Sans MM** and **Adobe Serif MM** must be in the Fonts folder in the System Folder. If you used the Installer to install either SuperATM, ATM 4.0 and above, or Acrobat, those items will be where they are supposed to be. If they're not and you want them, run the Installer again, or find the files on the original disk and copy those files to their respective holding places.

ATM Font Database

These items are what make ATM's font emulation work.

TrueType fonts

TrueType is a font technology developed several years ago by Apple. TrueType fonts are *not* PostScript or Type 1 (I'm assuming you **read** the information about PostScript fonts, pages 20–27).

TrueType fonts use *outlines* and thus are *scalable,* although they use a different type of mathematical outline formula from Post-Script (please see pages 20–21 for details on outlines and scaling).

If you use any version of Mac OS 8 or System 7, TrueType fonts will be displayed on your screen with smooth edges at any type size. The TrueType technology does basically the same thing as *Adobe Type Manager:* it goes to the outline data and *rasterizes* that outline (interprets the out-line) into the dots of the screen or of the printer. This means that TrueType fonts with *city names* such as Chicago will appear clean and smooth on your screen and printed on paper.

This is TrueType Chicago on the screen, 19 point. Looks pretty good, huh?

- *TrueType fonts are outline fonts.*
- *TrueType fonts are scalable.*
- *TrueType fonts are not PostScript, Type 1, or Type 3.*

TrueType icons

TrueType fonts are not made of two parts like PostScript fonts. Both the screen information and the printing information for TrueType are built into one unit so you have only one file to deal with. Although you can store TrueType files in *suitcases,* they are often seen floating around loose.

Palatino

This is the icon for a TrueType font. The three letter "A"s symbolize the fact that TrueType can be displayed and printed at all sizes.

So to use a TrueType font, the above icon is all you need. Store it wherever you store your fonts.

TrueType screen fonts?

You will probably see two different kinds of icons in your System Folder for some of the TrueType fonts. The other icons have only one "A" and their names include a point size (as shown below), which makes you think they are *bitmapped, fixed-size screen fonts,* right? Well, they are.

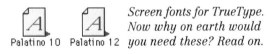
Palatino 10   Palatino 12

Screen fonts for TrueType. Now why on earth would you need these? Read on.

The icon with three letter "A"s on it is all the computer **needs** to create the TrueType font on the screen and for the printer. The other icons you may see, with a single "A" and labeled with a point size, are screen fonts in the sizes you will probably use the most.

If these screen fonts are installed, the Mac can display those particular sizes of that typeface faster (supposedly) and cleaner (truly) than if TrueType has to *rasterize* the printer font information.

These screen fonts do take up some room in your computer's memory and on your hard disk. If you don't mind the slight decrease in speed, which most of us would not even notice, you can eliminate all those various fixed-size icons for any of your **TrueType** fonts (but not for your PostScript fonts!). I do keep the sizes 10 and 12 for my city-named TrueType fonts because they seem to render more clearly on the screen, such as when I am word processing or browsing the web.

How do you tell TrueType screen fonts?

How can you tell if a fixed-size screen font was created to match a TrueType font or a PostScript font? I give up. I have searched high and low for an easy way to tell, and I have not found an answer, nor has anyone I have ever talked to. If you ever find out how to tell (besides having to use ResEdit), please let me know.

Advantages of TrueType

One advantage of TrueType is that you have only one icon to worry about. The other touted advantage of TrueType is that the type on your screen is clear and legible at any size, and you can print it clearly and legibly to any printer at any size.

What? Does that sound just like using PostScript fonts with *Adobe Type Manager*? Well, yes it does and that's true. See the next chapter for suggestions on determining which is the most appropriate technology for you to use.

Disadvantages of TrueType

TrueType fonts are larger in file size than PostScript fonts, so they take up more space on your disk and your documents can take longer to print. TrueType sometimes disagrees with PostScript laser printers for various technical reasons; newer printers have less trouble than older printers. If you have trouble printing TrueType to a PostScript printer, try changing the TrueType fonts to PostScript.

If you are going to send any documents to a service bureau for output from a PostScript imagesetter (all imagesetters are PostScript), don't use TrueType—the higher the resolution of the printer, the more trouble TrueType seems to cause.

TrueType and PostScript together

You can have the two technologies—TrueType and PostScript—living together in your computer. You can print documents that contain both TrueType and PostScript fonts. But there is one important rule to remember: ***do not keep two typefaces with the same name in your computer;*** that is, do not store TrueType *Times* and PostScript *Times* in your computer or you are asking for trouble. It might be trouble that never catches up with you, but I strongly recommend that for a clean, trouble-preventative system, don't keep two different faces with the same name in your Mac.

How do you know if you have both, and what do you do about it if you do? Well, if you have a *PostScript printer* (if you don't know, ask), move your TrueType Times, Helvetica, Symbol, Courier, and Palatino to an out-of-the-way place (like onto a floppy disk); remove both the TrueType icons and the screen fonts that you find in your Fonts folder (how-to details in Chapter 11). I keep a floppy disk called "TrueType Fonts" in which I store all of my TrueTypes in case I want them someday.

You see, you probably have certain TrueType fonts already installed in your Mac. Some of those fonts have the same names as *resident* PostScript fonts. Read on.

Yeah, so what if they have the same name?

So this, then, is what happens: You create a document with Times. You don't know at this point and you don't care whether it is PostScript or TrueType—it looks good on the screen. In actuality, though, this typeface is TrueType Times. When this document goes to a PostScript printer, the printer first looks in its own ROM (read-only memory, which is installed at the factory) for the *printer font* of this typeface. Lo and behold, it does find Times in its ROM, but it's PostScript Times! The printer doesn't care—if it finds a font with the same name, it uses that font.

But the *font metrics* in PostScript Times and those in TrueType Times are not the same (the font metrics are specifications built into the screen font that determine certain characteristics of the typeface, such as the stroke thickness, the space between letters, the thickness of the underline, etc.). So what you see on your screen and what is printed on paper will not always match!

Granted, Apple (who made the original TrueType Times) did try very hard to match the metrics of the PostScript Times so you will rarely see a difference between those two, but for clean font living and to prevent trouble, just clean it up—don't use any TrueType font that has the same name as one of your resident fonts.

On a PostScript printer, **you can never print any TrueType typeface that has the same name as one of the PostScript resident fonts** (see page 26 for info on resident fonts, if this concept is not perfectly clear).

What if the printer font is not in the ROM?

If the PostScript printer cannot find a printer font in its ROM with a matching name, it then looks in its RAM, then in an attached hard disk (if there is one), then it looks for Type 1 or Type 3 PostScript fonts in the System Folder, then for TrueType in the System Folder, then bitmaps in the System Folder. If it can't find what it needs, it looks in the same folder in which the screen font is stored (such as when you use a font management utility). The printer uses the first matching outline or bitmap it can find. And if it can't find what it needs anywhere, it uses Courier. (Actually, the *printer* itself doesn't look for it, but that's the general concept of how the process works.)

It is also possible to have two fonts of the same name if you use a font management utility (such as ATM Deluxe, Font Reserve, Suitcase, or MasterJuggler): perhaps you have your fonts stored outside your System Folder, but you didn't clean out your System Fonts folder, so there are some TrueType fonts with matching names still installed. You might have problems with your font management utility complaining about having two fonts open with the same name. If you organize your fonts as I suggest in Part III, however, you won't ever have this problem.

So should you use PostScript or TrueType?

PostScript or TrueType?

Well, I'm going to give you some suggestions here, but keep in mind that these are not Laws. You may find you have a personal preference that is different from mine or that you have a need for a certain technology that is different from what I suggest. That's okay! These are merely suggestions.

Also keep in mind that if you have a True-Type font and you need it to be Type 1 or vice versa, or a Windows font and you need it to be a Mac font, or just about any kind of conversion, you can use Macromedia Fontographer to convert them.

Suggestions

First of all, you must know whether or not you have a *PostScript printer.* If you don't know about yours, ask someone who does know (and read the section on PostScript printers and QuickDraw, non-PostScript printers, pages 12–13). If it cost much less than a thousand dollars, it's not PostScript. If it's color and it cost less than several thousand dollars, it's not PostScript.

If you have a QuickDraw printer

If you have a QuickDraw (non-PostScript) printer, you will probably be very happy with TrueType fonts. Or you could be just as happy with PostScript fonts and ATM. Or you could use both technologies in your computer at the same time. It's entirely up to you— choose what you feel happy with and what works for you.

If you have a PostScript printer

If you have a PostScript printer, you can use TrueType, but you may have fewer problems if you eliminate TrueType and stick to PostScript fonts and ATM. Now, I am a little hard on TrueType and you will find people who think TrueType is great. If you have had no trouble with TrueType, then use it. But if you are a professional-level designer and use PostScript graphics and create fine typography, I still suggest you use PostScript and ATM.

If you use a service bureau

Service bureaus use high-end PostScript imagesetters to "image" (print, output) the pages. The TrueType technology disagrees

with these imagesetters, and service bureau
operators generally prefer (many adamantly
insist) that you not bring TrueType into their
shops in your documents. If you want to use
TrueType in a job destined for a service
bureau, call the service bureau first and
ask permission. If they complain of trouble
printing TrueType, listen to them! They
know what they're talking about. There are
enough problems with imagesetting difficult
documents—don't add TrueType to the list.

Part II

Installing Fonts

This section deals with installing fonts into your System. You only need to read this section if you don't have very many fonts and you are **not** going to use a font management utility such as ATM Deluxe, Font Reserve, Suitcase, or MasterJuggler.

Now, you might use some of these programs for other things, such as making your fonts look better (ATM) or for managing other resources besides fonts (Suitcase or MasterJuggler). So please don't get confused when I mention using ATM Deluxe for font management, when you might already be using a non-deluxe version of ATM to make your fonts look beautiful on your screen.

Installing fonts

This section on installing fonts only applies to you if you are **not** using any of the font management utilities such as *ATM Deluxe, Suitcase, Font Reserve,* or *MasterJuggler.* If you use any one of those, then skip directly to page 51. If you don't know whether one of these utilities is installed or not, see below.

Should you use a font management utility?

If you have never bought or acquired more fonts for your Mac than what came installed, then no, you do not need a font management utility to help you manage fonts (although you might want one of these programs for the other things they do). An exception to this guideline would be if you bought a used Macintosh that was loaded with fonts. If there appears to be an excessive number of fonts on that machine, like 40 or 50, you should consider buying and learning to use *Adobe Type Manager **Deluxe version**, Suitcase, Font Reserve,* or *MasterJuggler.* Part III shows you how to use these programs.

Once you start collecting fonts, you will eventually find it necessary to learn to organize and manage them. Guaranteed.

Is a font management utility already installed?

How do you know if you have *ATM Deluxe, Suitcase, Font Reserve,* or *MasterJuggler* installed? Check the Apple menu. Their names might not be in alphabetical order, so check carefully, especially at the top of the list. (But just because it's installed doesn't mean it's actually being used for managing fonts!)

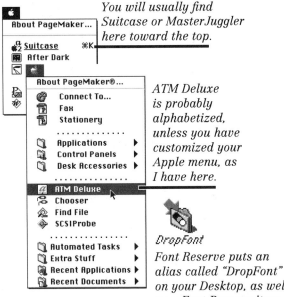

You will usually find Suitcase or MasterJuggler here toward the top.

ATM Deluxe is probably alphabetized, unless you have customized your Apple menu, as I have here.

Font Reserve puts an alias called "DropFont" on your Desktop, as well as a Font Reserve item in your Apple menu.

How many and which fonts are already installed?

How do you know how many fonts are already installed? A quick way to tell is to check Key Caps.

- From the Apple menu, choose Key Caps.
- When you see the keyboard layout on your screen, you will notice a new item in the menu bar, "Key Caps."
- Press on the new menu item "Key Caps" and you will get a list of the fonts that are open and ready to use.*

* If you do not use a font management utility, then what you see in Key Caps are the fonts that are installed directly in your System Folder/Fonts folder.

But, if you do use a font management utility, then what you see in Key Caps are all of the fonts that are loaded, or open, both from the System and from any font management utility in your Mac.

To find out which fonts are actually installed right into the System, look in the Fonts folder, which is inside the System Folder.

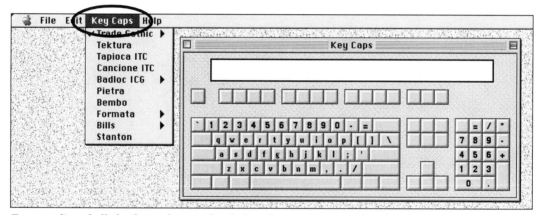

To see a list of all the fonts that are loaded at the moment, use Key Caps.

Installing fonts into the System

I'm assuming you read pages 11–42, that you have some version of Mac OS 8, you don't have a large number of fonts, and you are not using a font management utility.

Before you install

Close all windows except your hard disk window. Make sure the System Folder is closed. You should see the System Folder and it should look like this:

System Folder

If you usually view your window as some kind of list, of course that will work also. You can certainly install fonts into the System Folder when it looks like this:

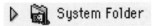

*If you're using **System 7.1 through 7.6**, you will have to first **quit** all open applications before you can install fonts into the System Folder.*

Now you need to find the fonts you want to install. You don't want the open window of the fonts disk to hide the System Folder. Just arrange things on your screen so you can see the System Folder and you can also see the window that holds your fonts.

If the new fonts are on a floppy disk, this process will install *copies* of the fonts. Then you can store the floppy disk with the original fonts in a safe place; you may need those originals again if the installed fonts ever get corrupted or damaged, which is not unusual.

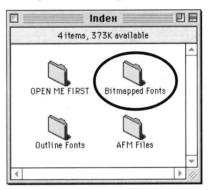

This is an example of a new disk of fonts. They don't all look like this, but you will find these elements.

*Often you will see TrueType versions and Type 1 PostScript versions of the same font on the same disk. **Don't install both!** Choose one format (see pages 41–42 if you don't know which format to choose).*

Installing screen fonts

Remember, PostScript fonts come in pairs (pages 20–25). You need to install both parts of the pairs, the screen fonts and the printer fonts.

Let's do the screen fonts first. You can do it any of the following ways. Each method will prompt a dialog box that will ask permission to put the file where it belongs; you just click OK:

> ⚠ **These items need to be stored in the Fonts folder in order to be available to the computer. Put these items into the Fonts folder?**
>
> [Cancel] [**OK**]

Installing TrueType

If it's a TrueType font, just drag the TrueType icon over to the closed System Folder and drop it on top of the folder. You're done.

Now this TrueType icon, as you already know, is not really a screen font, but since it includes the screen fonts within the file, we're installing it here.

Palatino

Drop this icon onto the closed System Folder.

Installing PostScript fonts

You can drag an entire suitcase onto the System Folder. Remember, the suitcase contains the bitmapped screen fonts that are only one-half of what you need for a PostScript font pair.

Index.bmap

Drop this icon onto the closed System Folder.

But: You really should open the suitcase first (double-click on it) and see what's inside before you drop it on the System Folder.

> If you're using any version of ATM, you need to install only **one point size** of each individual font; don't waste space by installing the 9, 10, 12, 14, 18, 24, and 36 sizes of every font!

You can install the individual bitmaps into the System Folder if you like.

If there are more than two bitmaps in the family, leave them in the suitcase. Before (or after) you drop that suitcase on the System Folder, though, remove the extra bitmap sizes from the suitcase.

Index 24

*In this example, there are four different fonts (Index Bold, Index Book, Index Book Expert, and Index Book Italic). There are two sizes of each font. You only need to install **one size** of each, so toss the 12-point versions either before or after you put the suitcase in the System Folder.*

Installing outline printer fonts

If you're installing **TrueType fonts,** there are no printer fonts to install so you can go back to your coffee break now.

If you're installing **PostScript fonts,** you understand about printer fonts because you read pages 20–25, right? Unlike a suitcase or a screen font, which always looks like a suitcase or a screen font, printer icons have all kinds of shapes and looks. See page 25 for eight different examples.

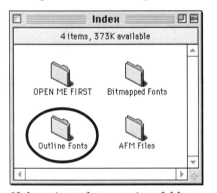

If the printer fonts are in a folder, open the folder and make sure you have one printer font for each bitmapped font that you just installed. If any bitmap is missing a printer font (or vice versa), the font will not function!

Inside the folder on this disk are four printer fonts (shown below), one for each of the four bitmaps we installed on the previous page. This is good.

Once you have found the printer fonts on your disk, all you need to do to install them is drag them onto the closed System Folder. As usual, you'll get a little message asking if the Mac should put them where they belong and you just agree (click OK). That's it.

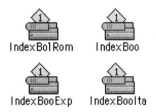

If you install four different screen fonts, such as Index Bold Roman, Index Book, Index Book Expert, and Index Book Italic, then you must install four matching printer fonts.

After you install

When you drop any of these items onto the System Folder, you will get a message something like this:

> The font suitcase "Index.bmap" will not be available to currently running applications until they have quit.
>
> OK

*This is a silly message—the fonts won't be available to an open application until it has **quit**? What it means to say is that if you have an application open when you install fonts, the new fonts won't appear in that application's font menu until you have **quit and relaunched** the application. (Some applications, however, such as PageMaker, are smart enough to find the newly installed font instantly.)*

In any version of System 7, you can't install fonts if any application is open anyway, so you won't get this message.

Don't install AFM or .fog files

When you have a new font to install, you will often see files with extensions of ".afm" or perhaps ".fog" in the folder along with the new font. The .afm file contains a text version of the *font metrics*. You do not need to install this! The .fog file is a database that Fontographer builds when someone creates a new font in that program. You don't need to install the .fog file either.

Scarlett.AFM   Rapture.fog

Where did the files go?

The Mac puts both the screen fonts and the printer fonts into a folder called **Fonts,** which is of course in the System Folder. You can actually put the fonts directly in the Fonts folder yourself. If you ever need ***to remove fonts,*** simply open the Fonts folder and drag them out.

Fonts

The Fonts folder actually holds both portions of PostScript fonts (the screen fonts and the matching printer fonts), as well as TrueType.

The process, visually

So here is an example of a font disk and how to install the fonts from it.

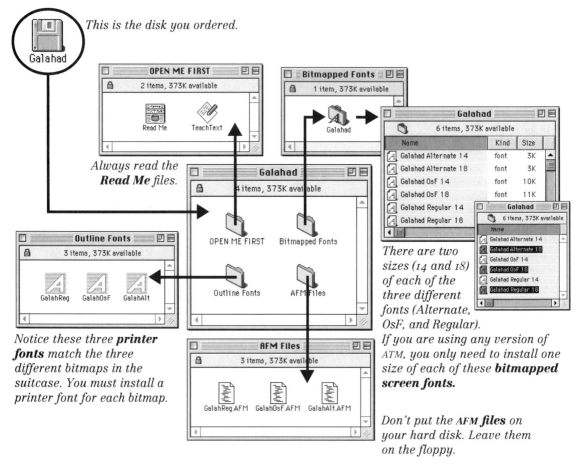

This is the disk you ordered.

Always read the ***Read Me*** *files.*

Notice these three ***printer fonts*** *match the three different bitmaps in the suitcase. You must install a printer font for each bitmap.*

There are two sizes (14 and 18) of each of the three different fonts (Alternate, OsF, and Regular). If you are using any version of ATM, *you only need to install one size of each of these* ***bitmapped screen fonts.***

Don't put the AFM ***files*** *on your hard disk. Leave them on the floppy.*

Drag these three bitmapped screen fonts (one size of each) and drop them on the closed System Folder. Then drag the three matching printer font icons onto the Stystem Folder. Done.

Or drag the entire suitcase to the System Folder and drop it, instead of dragging the individual bitmaps. (You might want to remove the excess bitmaps from the suitcase before you install the entire suitcase.)

Part III Font Management

Before you can successfully use a font management utility, you must first organize your fonts. This will take some time, but you have to do it. It's actually kind of fun, and you will be amazed at how much hard disk space you'll have after you toss unnecessary files, and how much better you will understand your fonts. Then when you use a font management utility, it will all make such good sense.

How to organize your fonts

You only need to read and follow the directions in this chapter if you have a large number of fonts . . .
What is a "large number"? I'd say once you have bought or acquired about ten to fifteen additional families, you are ready to learn how to manage them. You've read directions that tell you to stick all your fonts in the System Folder, but don't believe 'em. I, for instance, have several hundred megabytes of fonts. Can you imagine what would happen if I dropped all those fonts into my System Folder?

. . . AND if you plan to use a font management utility. The following chapters tell you about each of the four font management utilities available to you. All of these utilities let you store your fonts in a folder anywhere on your hard disk and open just the ones you need, when you need to use them. The advantage is that, although the fonts will still take up hard disk space, only the fonts you actually load will take up RAM (memory), your font menu will be shorter and more manageble, plus you can have an unlimited number of fonts at your disposal, rather than the limit imposed by the System. (Some of these utilities have other features besides font management, but that's not the focus of this book.)

First: Make sure you know these things

Before you begin

Before we start talking about managing fonts, I'm assuming you have **read** the previous part of this book, the font technology part. Can you identify the icons below? If you can't, please go back and read the first section of this book. Otherwise you may not only be confused, you may mess things up worse than they already are. You need to know:

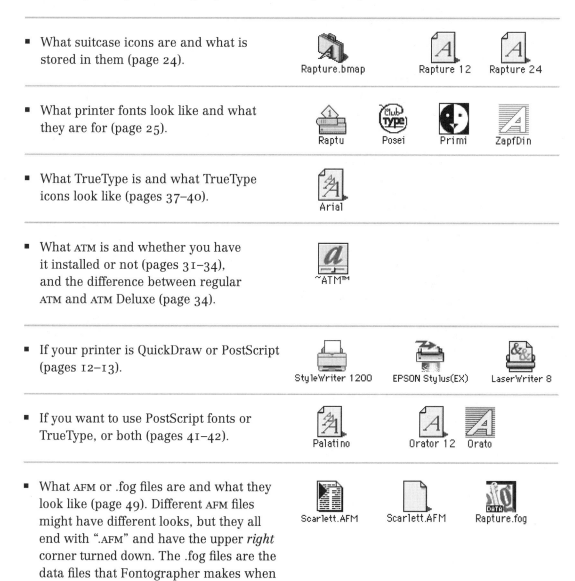

- What suitcase icons are and what is stored in them (page 24).

  Rapture.bmap   Rapture 12   Rapture 24

- What printer fonts look like and what they are for (page 25).

  Raptu   Posei   Primi   ZapfDin

- What TrueType is and what TrueType icons look like (pages 37–40).

  Arial

- What ATM is and whether you have it installed or not (pages 31–34), and the difference between regular ATM and ATM Deluxe (page 34).

  ~ATM™

- If your printer is QuickDraw or PostScript (pages 12–13).

  StyleWriter 1200   EPSON Stylus(EX)   LaserWriter 8

- If you want to use PostScript fonts or TrueType, or both (pages 41–42).

  Palatino   Orator 12   Orato

- What AFM or .fog files are and what they look like (page 49). Different AFM files might have different looks, but they all end with ".AFM" and have the upper *right* corner turned down. The .fog files are the data files that Fontographer makes when you create a font.

  Scarlett.AFM   Scarlett.AFM   Rapture.fog

Next: Clean up the fonts in your System Folder

Clean up

You can have TrueType and PostScript fonts in your computer, but never two fonts from the two different technologies *with the same name*. When you install a new Macintosh System in your computer, it replaces any existing screen fonts for Times, Helvetica, Courier, Symbol, and sometimes Palatino; it replaces any screen fonts that it found that had those same names. When you install Adobe Type Manager, it replaces any TrueType Times, Helvetica, Courier, and Symbol with PostScript versions. So it doesn't take long for things to get all mixed up in your Fonts folder (the one in your System Folder).

What we're going to do first is clean up the fonts that are stored somewhere in your System Folder so you'll have consistent screen fonts that match what you print.

We're also going to remove any other fonts you may have installed in your System, in preparation for organizing them to be managed by a utility.

Assumptions!

Now, I do have to assume that if you have a *PostScript printer* you have the disk that came with your printer that contains the *screen fonts;* these screen fonts match the *resident fonts* that are already installed in your printer.

I assume, even if you have a *non-PostScript printer,* that if you use PostScript fonts you also use ATM (which you really, really must; it's silly not to use ATM if you use PostScript fonts), and that you have the ATM disk containing the screen and printer fonts.

If not, don't throw anything away unless you know you have a backup somewhere, or you know you absolutely don't need it.

I make a folder called something like "Toss These?" and store files in there until I feel comfortable actually throwing them into the trash can.

Toss These?

Step 1: Make new folders

So, first you need to make some folders
in preparation for housecleaning.

- Quit all applications.

- On your hard disk somewhere, but not in
  the System Folder, make a folder and name
  it "TrueType Fonts."

TrueType Fonts

- Make another folder on your hard disk and
  name it "Temporary Font Storage." This
  folder is only for the intermediate process
  in the clean-up; when we're done, you'll
  throw this folder away.

Temporary Font Storage

- Make another folder on your hard disk and
  name it "My Good Fonts." Do not put this
  in your System Folder! Leave it right at the
  top level of your hard disk or sitting on
  your Desktop.

My Good Fonts

- Make another folder on your hard disk and
  name it "Missing Font Files." In this folder
  you'll store any fonts that are missing
  critical matches. Don't throw them away
  because the missing part might appear
  later. If the missing parts never appear,
  you'll have to throw these away, or at
  least store them off your hard disk.

Missing Font Files

- If you haven't already, make a folder
  called "Toss These?" in which to store
  files that you plan to throw away later.

Toss These?

*You could put all of these extra folders inside
the one folder Temporary Font Storage, just
to keep everything neat. It's up to you.*

Step 2: Move your fonts to the Temporary Font Storage folder

- Move all of the fonts from the **Fonts** folder (the one in the System Folder) and put them all in the **Temporary Font Storage** folder. In a minute, we are going to move some of these fonts back into the Fonts folder, some into the TrueType Folder, some into the Toss These folder, and we are going to organize the rest into the folder called My Good Fonts. But for now, put everything into the Temporary Font Storage folder.

Now, if you "Select All" and try to drag the fonts out of the Fonts folder, the Mac will probably yell at you, warning you that you can't remove either Chicago or Charcoal (whichever one is the System font) and the font that you have chosen to view your Desktop in (which is probably Geneva, unless you have changed it).* So do this:

- Select All (Command A).

- Hold down the Shift key and click on Chicago or Charcoal (or both) and Geneva.

- Let go of the Shift key, then press on *one* of the selected, highlighted icons and drag, which will drag *all* of the selected fonts to the Temporary Font Storage folder.

If you are running Mac OS 8 and don't know what your Desktop view font is, go to the Desktop and check the Preferences, under the Edit menu. If you are on some version of System 7, check the Views control panel.

Inside the System Folder is the official Fonts folder.

System Folder   Fonts

Your Fonts folder inside your System Folder won't look exactly like this, but it will be similar.

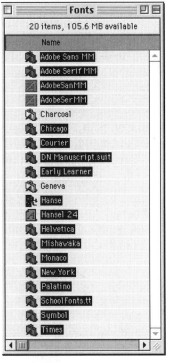

Leave the System font, which might be Charcoal or Chicago, and leave Geneva in your Fonts folder. Move the rest to the Temporary Fonts Storage folder.

If you want, go ahead and leave the other city-named fonts in this folder. I do. Open the suitcases to make sure they are TrueType.

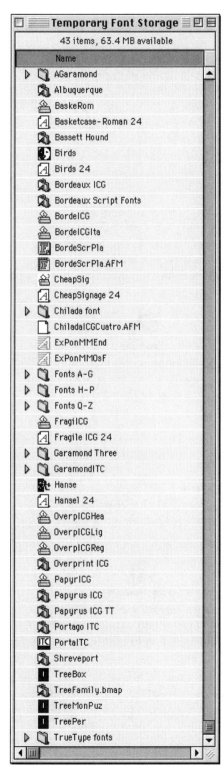

Temporary Font Storage
43 items, 63.4 MB available

Name
▷ AGaramond
Albuquerque
BaskeRom
Basketcase-Roman 24
Bassett Hound
Birds
Birds 24
Bordeaux ICG
Bordeaux Script Fonts
BordeICG
BordeICGIta
BordeScrPla
BordeScrPla.AFM
CheapSig
CheapSignage 24
▷ Chilada font
ChiladaICGCuatro.AFM
ExPonMMEnd
ExPonMMOsF
▷ Fonts A-G
▷ Fonts H-P
▷ Fonts Q-Z
FragiICG
Fragile ICG 24
▷ Garamond Three
▷ GaramondITC
Hanse
Hansel 24
OverpICGHea
OverpICGLig
OverpICGReg
Overprint ICG
PapyrICG
Papyrus ICG
Papyrus ICG TT
Portago ITC
PortalTC
Shreveport
TreeBox
TreeFamily.bmap
TreeMonPuz
TreePer
▷ TrueType fonts

Gather up all the fonts from all over your hard disk and put them in this Temporary Font Storage folder. You might find fonts in application folders, in your System Folder floating around loose, in folders tucked deep within other folders, anywhere. Put them all in here and spend the time to organize them.

This folder is a mess, yes? Look at all the different Garamonds (choose one version and toss the rest, or at least store them out of the way and clearly labeled); look at all the parts that don't match; look at the AFM files; and who knows how many fonts are inside the folders called "Fonts A-G" and so on and so on.

Selectively and purposefully return some fonts

Step 3: Put some fonts back into the Fonts folder in the System Folder

There are a couple of fonts that *must* stay in the Fonts folder, and there are others that you might *want* to leave in there:

- The two suitcases called **Adobe Serif MM** and **Adobe Sans MM,** plus their matching printer fonts, must be in the Fonts folder if you want ATM to do its font emulation trick (page 36). If you don't have those two Adobe suitcases, don't worry about it—they are not critical to anything except font emulation, and if you've been living without it anyway, why worry.

Adobe Serif MM   AdobeSerMM

Adobe Sans MM   AdobeSanMM

If you do want ATM to do font emulation, these files must stay in the Fonts folder in the System Folder.

- I keep the city-named TrueType fonts in my Fonts folder just because I like to have them around all the time for word processing and web browsing. (But *instead* of keeping them in the Fonts folder, you *could* make a set of city-named TrueType fonts and only open them when you need them.)

Geneva   New York

In Netscape, I set my font default to Geneva or New York because it is so much easier to read on the screen.

- I always keep PostScript versions (because I have a PostScript printer) of Zapf Dingbats and Symbol in my Fonts folder because I always want them accessible and I don't want to bother to make a set for them.

Zapf Dingbats 12   ZapfDin

Both the screen font and its matching printer font must be in the same folder.

- If you have an encyclopedia on CD-ROM that your kids use all the time, or some other kids' program that installed bitmap fonts into your Fonts folder, you might want to leave those in there so your kids don't have to know how to use the font management utility to get the fonts for their program.

Early Learner   SchoolFonts.tt

These fonts get installed with ClarisWorks for Kids. To keep things easy, go ahead and leave fonts like this in the Fonts folder in the System Folder.

- Do not put AFM files or .fog files in the Fonts folder! Don't even put them in the System Folder.

Scarlett.AFM   Scarlett.AFM   Rapture.fog

Check 'em out first

You need to open suitcases and check them out before you put them back into the Fonts folder in the System Folder.

New York

*Let's say you want to keep **New York** in your Fonts folder. You can take this entire suitcase back over to the Fonts folder, or you can take just the icon with the three A's on it. If you use New York much, you might want to keep the entire suitcase with the extra bitmaps so those fixed sizes are clearer on the screen.*

Symbol

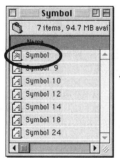

*If you have a **PostScript printer,** would you want to keep this **TrueType** version of **Symbol** in your Fonts folder? No! Remember, Symbol is a resident font (page 26).*

*But if you have a **non-PostScript printer,** go ahead and keep this in your Fonts folder, but then don't install the PostScript version of Symbol as well!*

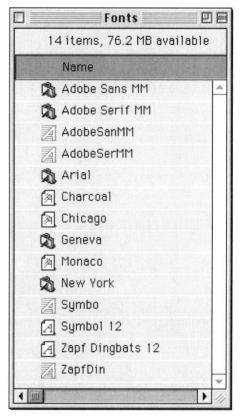

So this is how my Fonts folder in my System Folder appears. Yours may be different because you will customize it to suit the way you work.

Notice I keep Symbol and Zapf Dingbats in my System Folder. I keep them there because I always want them accessible. I could choose to permanently open them through my font management utility instead of storing them here.

Then: Organize your TrueType fonts

Step 4: Separate the TrueType fonts from the PostScript fonts

The point of separating TrueType from PostScript is to make sure you don't have fonts of the same name from each technology. It's easy to end up with fonts of the same name because when you buy a disk of fonts the vendor gives you both TrueType and PostScript so you can choose.

- Move all of your TrueType fonts into the folder you made earlier called TrueType Fonts. You might have to open suitcases to see whether a TrueType icon is inside.

- Once you have all of the TrueType fonts in one place, the most important thing to check is whether you have TrueType and PostScript versions of the same font.

  Compare the two folders (the Temporary Fonts Folder and the TrueType Fonts Folder). Are there typefaces with the same name? You need to make a decision—do you keep the TrueType or the PostScript version?

  As you've already read, if you have a PostScript printer (pages 12–13) it is best to keep the PostScript fonts and use Adobe Type Manager so the type appears smooth on the screen.

  If you have a non-PostScript printer, you can choose to either keep the TrueType version, or the PostScript versions as long as you use Adobe Type Manager.

  If you ever plan to send your files to a service bureau, then get rid of the TrueType and keep only the PostScript, no matter which kind of printer you have.

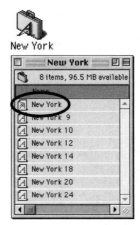

New York

You won't find any printer fonts for this typeface because it is TrueType. The only file in this suitcase you really need is the one called New York (circled), but it will appear a little clearer on your screen in the fixed sizes if you keep them installed. I keep the 10, 12, and 14 points installed because I use them for word processing and web browsing.

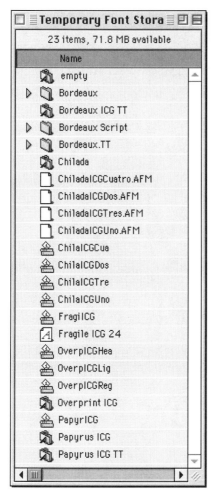

Temporary Font Stora		
23 items, 71.8 MB available		
Name		

- empty
- ▷ Bordeaux
- Bordeaux ICG TT
- ▷ Bordeaux Script
- ▷ Bordeaux.TT
- Chilada
- ChiladaICGCuatro.AFM
- ChiladaICGDos.AFM
- ChiladaICGTres.AFM
- ChiladaICGUno.AFM
- ChilaICGCua
- ChilaICGDos
- ChilaICGTre
- ChilaICGUno
- FragiICG
- Fragile ICG 24
- OverpICGHea
- OverpICGLig
- OverpICGReg
- Overprint ICG
- PapyrICG
- Papyrus ICG
- Papyrus ICG TT

TrueType Fonts

Question: *So which of the files in this Temporary Font Storage folder should be moved over into the TrueType Fonts folder?*

_____

_____

_____

Clues:

- *The vendors (or maybe you) have put a "TT" at the end of the suitcase file name to indicate TrueType fonts. That's a good habit.*

- *If you see printer fonts with the same name as a suitcase or bitmap, you can be fairly confident that the printer and suitcase/bitmap are the two parts of the PostScript font.*

Answer: So from this collection, you should move *Bordeaux ICG TT, Bordeaux.TT,* and *Papyrus ICG TT* into the TrueType Fonts folder. Make a decision about whether to keep these TrueTypes or not, based on your printer, whether you plan to use a service bureau, and whether or not you have PostScript versions of these same fonts.

OK, now: Organize the rest of your fonts

Step 5: Do the big job

Okay, so all you've got left in that Temporary Fonts Storage folder is a bunch of PostScript fonts. Now you are ready to organize these fonts so you will always know exactly where they all are, they will be easy to access and open, and conveniently arranged so you can gather them easily for transporting to your service bureau. At the end of this process you will have a folder like the one shown on the right: each family in a separate folder, and each family folder containing the screen fonts and matching printer fonts for that family.

Yes, I know all this rearranging might take some time, depending on how you have been managing your fonts previously. Truly, though, the time spent is well worth it.

- You've still got that folder on your hard disk (not inside your System Folder!) called "My Good Fonts," right? (When you're done organizing everything, you can rename it anything you want.) You're going to transfer fonts from the Temporary Font Storage folder into that one.

My Good Fonts

This is what you are going to do now: organize your fonts into families and those families into folders.

This is the actual folder where I store the fonts I keep on my hard disk (I have others elsewhere). Notice I made one folder called "Scripts"; it holds a variety of scripts, since most scripts only have one member in the family.

I also have one folder that contains all of my TrueType fonts, since I own very few and never use them anyway.

Your fonts folder will look similar to this, but not exactly the same, of course.

- So you're going to check every font file in the Temporary Fonts Storage folder. You'll make a separate folder for each of the font families you own. When a folder is complete with its entire family and all its matching pairs, you can move the family folder into My Good Fonts folder.

You might want to make one folder that holds all your scripts, as in the illustration above right. If you have some really wild fonts you only use occasionally, you might want to store all of them in one folder called "Wild Fonts." If you have a collection of related fonts that you often use together, such as the Stone clan (Stone Sans, Stone Informal, and Stone Serif), make one "Stone" folder and store all three families inside, with one suitcase per family. I'll walk you through it.

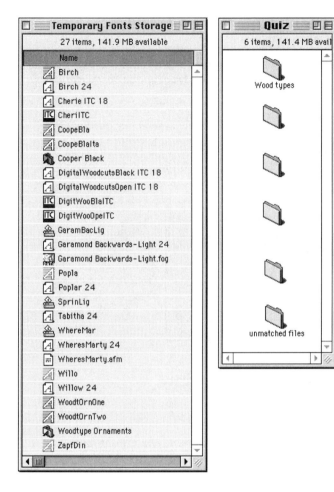

Temporary Fonts Storage
27 items, 141.9 MB available

Name
Birch
Birch 24
Cherie ITC 18
CheriITC
CoopeBla
CoopeBlaIta
Cooper Black
DigitalWoodcutsBlack ITC 18
DigitalWoodcutsOpen ITC 18
DigitWooBlaITC
DigitWooOpeITC
GaramBacLig
Garamond Backwards-Light 24
Garamond Backwards-Light.fog
Popla
Poplar 24
SprinLig
Tabitha 24
WhereMar
WheresMarty 24
WheresMarty.afm
Willo
Willow 24
WoodtOrnOne
WoodtOrnTwo
Woodtype Ornaments
ZapfDin

Quiz
6 items, 141.4 MB avail

Wood types

unmatched files

Okay, here's another little quiz for you:

Study the Temporary Fonts Storage folder (to the far left).

Based on the font files you see, decide what to name the empty folders in the Quiz folder.

Draw lines from the files in the Temporary Fonts Storage folder to the newly named folders in the Quiz folder where they should be stored.

If you would like to organize it differently, feel free to add another folder or two.

Hint: The "Wood types" folder already set up for you could contain all the fonts that have tree (wood) names, plus related fonts.

Question 1: Which font would show up in the font menu in your application, but would never print properly? Why would it show up and why would it not print properly?

Question 2: Which two fonts might print properly, but you wouldn't be able to use them in the first place because they wouldn't appear in your font menu? Why?

Question 3: Which two files don't need to be stored on your hard disk at all?

1: Tabitha would appear in the font menu because its screen font is here. But it wouldn't print properly because there is no matching printer font.

2: Spring Light (SprinLig) and Zapf Dingbats would theoretically print properly because the printer fonts are available, but they would never appear in the font menu because there are no matching screen fonts.

3: You don't need to keep the AFM file for WheresMarty, or the .fog file for Garamond Backwards-Light.

Keep families together

Start with the easy stuff—move families into the family folders

Start with the fonts that are easy matches, the ones whose suitcase and printer fonts are both visible and available.

The only items allowed into My Good Fonts folder are folders that contain whole, healthy families, either TrueType or PostScript pairs.

- So make a family font folder inside the Temporary Fonts Storage folder. Let's say you have the font Leawood; make a new folder called "Leawood." Then find the Leawood suitcase.

This is the folder inside of the Temporary Fonts Storage folder, waiting for its family to be placed inside.

- Open the Leawood suitcase (double-click on it). Drag to the trash every screen font *except* one size of each family member. If the largest size you have is 12-point, then leave the 12-point. If this is a decorative typeface, instead of the 12-point screen font, store a larger size, such as 18-, 24-, or even 36-point.

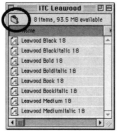

All that should be in the family suitcase is one fixed-size screen font for each member of the family.

- Now check to see that you have one printer font for each family member you see in the suitcase. If there are eight bitmaps in the suitcase, you should have eight printer fonts outside the suitcase.

  If any file is unmatched, put it in the Missing Font Files folder!

Make sure you have one printer font for each bitmap member of the family.

- Now move both the suitcase and the matching printer fonts into the family folder that you made. That typeface is now good and healthy and will always work.

  Drag the Leawood family folder into My Good Fonts folder.

  Organize the rest of the fonts into My Good Fonts folder in the same way.

Now the Leawood family folder, with its eight bitmaps in the suitcase and its eight matching printer fonts, is ready to go into My Good Fonts.

- Don't forget to put Times, Helvetica, Symbol, and Courier into My Good Fonts folder, whether you use TrueType or PostScript.

If you're using ATM, you'll find the PostScript printer fonts for these typefaces on the ATM disk (if they're not already installed).

Making new suitcases: when, why, and how

- You might have **more than one suitcase** for the family. If you have several suitcases, such as a suitcase for the main family and another suitcase for the expanded and condensed versions, or perhaps for the expert collection, you might want to combine them into one suitcase.

  Or you might have **no existing suitcases** (just a collection of bitmaps). If the family has more than one bitmap, you should make a suitcase for them, as follows:

These can be combined into one suitcase. Just drag one suitcase and drop it into the other.

Rather than float individually, put these three family members into one suitcase.

You can use a menu command in your font management utility to make a new, empty suitcase, but sometimes it's easier to duplicate an existing suitcase and then empty it.

❶ Find a suitcase. Click once on it.

❷ Press Command D to duplicate it.

❸ Rename the new suitcase "Empty" (type the new name *before you click;* if you already clicked somewhere and the border disappeared, click on the duplicate's *name* again, then type).

❹ Double-click on this suitcase to open its window. Press Command A to select all the items, then drag them all to the trash. Close the window. Empty trash.

Or press Command Delete to trash the selected items; or hold down the Control key and press on one of the selected items, then choose "Move To Trash" from the menu that pops up.

Now you have an empty suitcase. Make several copies of the empty suitcase so they are ready when you need them.

- Now when you drag this Empty suitcase into one of the family folders, *hold down the Option key while you drag.* This will put a *copy* of the Empty suitcase into the family folder.

- So, *when necessary,* you'll put an empty suitcase into a folder. When necessary, into that suitcase you'll put just one bitmap for each family member.

Combine family members into one suitcase, where appropriate

- If you have **several existing suitcases that belong to one family,** you should probably **combine** all the **suitcases** into one suitcase (unless the family is huge, like over twenty separate members).

  ❶ Take a look at the family members. Can they be combined because they are all variants of one family? (For instance, if you have several Garamond *families* from different vendors—they would have slightly different names—you would **not** combine them into one suitcase.)

  ❷ Make a Bordeaux family folder.

  ❸ Inside the folder, make an empty suitcase (page 65) and give it the family name.

  ❹ Open the existing suitcases.

  ❺ Drag one bitmap of each member (bold, italic, regular, etc.) into the new, empty suitcase, as shown.

❶

	Temporary Font Storage		
25 items, 72 MB available			
Name	Size	Kind	
empty	17K	font suitcase	
Bordeaux ICG	50K	font suitcase	
Bordeaux Script Fonts	66K	font suitcase	
BordeICG	50K	PostScript™ font	
BordeICGIta	50K	PostScript™ font	
BordeScrPla	66K	PostScript™ font	
BordeScrPla.AFM	33K	document	
Chilada	50K	font suitcase	

You can see two separate suitcases for the face Bordeaux, one for the regular font and one for the script version. You can see three printer fonts (notice in the window under "Kind" they are labeled "PostScript™ font," which is your clue that they are all printer fonts, even though the icons are not the same). You also see an AFM file—do you need to keep that on your hard disk? No.

The three printer fonts are a clue that one of those suitcases must have two different family members inside of it. Let's combine the two suitcases into one family suitcase.

❷

Bordeaux

Make a Bordeaux family folder in the folder named My Good Fonts.

❸

	Bordeaux		
1 item, 71.5 MB available			
	Bordeaux.bmp		

Inside this family folder, make an empty suitcase, and rename it. You might want to add "screen" or "bmap" at the end of the name so you can tell what it is without the icon.

❹
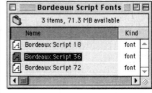

Bordeaux ICG   Bordeaux Script Fonts

	Bordeaux ICG		
10 items, 71.5 MB avail			
Name			
Bordeaux ICG 10			
Bordeaux ICG 12			
Bordeaux ICG 14			
Bordeaux ICG 18			
Bordeaux ICG 24			
Bordeaux ICG Italic 10			
Bordeaux ICG Italic 12			
Bordeaux ICG Italic 14			
Bordeaux ICG Italic 18			
Bordeaux ICG Italic 24			

	Bordeaux Script Fonts		
3 items, 71.3 MB available			
Name		Kind	
Bordeaux Script 18		font	
Bordeaux Script 36		font	
Bordeaux Script 72		font	

Take a look in each of the existing suitcases. You don't need all those extra bitmaps, do you? Just take one bitmap from each family and drag it to the new Bordeaux.bmp suitcase, as shown in ❺, below.

❺

Bordeaux.bmp

	Bordeaux.bmp		
3 items, 71.2 MB available			
Name		Kind	
Bordeaux ICG 24		font	
Bordeaux ICG Italic 24		font	
Bordeaux Script 36		font	

If there are three bitmap family members, you need three printer fonts to match, right?

	Bordeaux		
4 items, 70.9 MB available			
Name			
Bordeaux.bmp			
BordeICG			
BordeICGIta			
BordeScrPla			

Here is the whole, healthy Bordeaux family folder, with the fonts ready to use.

When not to combine fonts into one suitcase

You don't *always* want to combine entire families into one suitcase. Your font management utility will open entire suitcases and load all of the fonts contained in that entire suitcase with the click of one button. For just this reason you want to be careful about how much you put into each suitcase. (Font Reserve does let you open individual fonts, even though you've stored them in suitcases.)

- If a family is extremely large, like the Universe family, you might want to use two or three suitcases. But try to combine the fonts in the suitcases in combinations that you might use together; that is, combine light weights with heavy weights, rather than all the heavy weights together.

- You might have multiple master fonts or expert sets, or even a multiple master expert set. Sometimes in a document you want the plain ol' font and sometimes you want the whole shebang, multiples and experts. If you put all of the various fonts into one suitcase, you'll have to open them all every time you use that typeface. If you separate the regular family from the expert family, you can choose to open just one, the other, or both.

- You don't want all of your scripts to be in one suitcase because you don't usually use more than one script at a time, right? So if you leave each script separate, but in one folder (as shown to the right), you can choose to open individual scripts instead of one suitcase that contains every script you own.

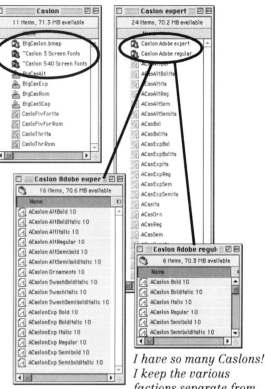

I have so many Caslons! I keep the various factions separate from each other.

I keep all of my scripts in one folder, but I leave the individual bitmaps loose instead of grouping them all into one suitcase. This way I can open each individual script one at a time.

Congratulate yourself!

The finished product

- When you are finished, you should have a folder called "My Good Fonts," and in this folder you should have a collection of other folders, each with the name of a font family or perhaps a group of families. Inside each family folder should be a suitcase of screen fonts and their matching printer fonts (unless it is TrueType, in which case you will have no printer fonts).

  I also keep an empty suitcase in here called "Blank," ready any time I may need an empty suitcase.

- Store this entire folder on your hard disk, anywhere except inside the System Folder.

  When you acquire new fonts, follow the same process as when you cleaned up:

  ☐ Make a new folder inside My Good Fonts.

  ☐ Copy the font suitcase (if there is one) to the folder, and remove all but one of the fixed-size bitmaps. (If the family consists of only one font, you might not have a suitcase, but just one bitmap.)

  ☐ Copy matching printer fonts from the disk into the same folder (or if it's TrueType, just drop the TrueType icon into the folder).

How simple it really is!

Okay—now you are ready to use your font management utility!

This is where I store my fonts folder, on the top level of my hard disk. It's important to name it something other than "Fonts" so you never get it confused with the Fonts folder that is kept in the System Folder.

How to manage your fonts

Okay. We're at the final phase of managing your fonts. I assume you have organized all of your fonts. If you haven't, you really must go back through the previous chapter and organize every font you own before you try to use a font management utility.

So what does a font management utility do for you?

Well, if you *don't* use a font management utility, you know what happens, right? All of your fonts are available all the time. This is fine if you have a small number of fonts (like fewer than 15 to 20 different *families*). But once you start collecting them you don't want all your fonts open all the time because they clog up your memory, they make things run slower, there is a maximum number of fonts that can be installed into the System, and some people (who, me?) have so many fonts that if they were all installed the computer would just choke and die.

So by using a font management utility you can store your fonts on your hard disk and open just the selected fonts you need for the current project. When you don't need those anymore, you can close them with the click of a button and open others. It's too cool. And indispensable besides.

Make sure you have the latest versions of everything—your software applications, your font management utility of choice, Adobe Type Manager, Adobe Type Reunion (if you use it), etc.—or you can run into all kinds of strange problems. In fact, if you have problems, that's the first thing to check—make sure you have current versions of everything.

What are your choices?

There are four font management utilities on the market right now. Two have been around for a long time; two are new. In this chapter I'll show you what each of these utilities looks like, how it works, its advantages and disadvantages, and you can decide which one would be best for you. These are the four we'll look at:

p. 71 Adobe Type Manager Deluxe
from Adobe Systems, Inc.
(The Deluxe version is different from plain ol' Adobe Type Manager! See page 34.)

p. 76 Suitcase from Symantec Corporation

p. 85 MasterJuggler from Alsoft, Inc.

p. 95 Font Reserve from DiamondSoft, Inc.

You need to choose **one** of these! **Only one!** You will have problems if you install more than one font management utility.

The advantage of sets

Each of the font management utilities allows you to make *sets* of your fonts. A set is simply a list of fonts. You can create a separate set of fonts for each project you work on. Because the set is simply a list of font names, you can have the same font in many different sets (kind of like an alias, if you understand how aliases work).

The sets are what make these utilities so incredibly useful (besides the fact that you don't have to keep your fonts in the System Folder). For instance, I have a set called "Fax" because I can never remember what fonts I use in my fax cover sheet. I have a set for each of my books, for my bio, for articles that need special typefaces, for each presentation, for my user group newsletter, for different web sites I am creating, etc. When I am about to work on a project, I simply open the set for that project. When I change projects, with the click of a button I can put those fonts away and open another set, often without even quitting my application (PageMaker and QuarkXPress update the font menu instantly).

One of the most important features you will learn to use in your chosen utility is how to make, open, and close these sets of fonts.

How do you use a font management utility?

Your fonts need to be organized first. You can store them all loose in one folder, or if you have more than a few fonts, store each family in a separate folder that contains the bitmap and outline pairs (unless they're TrueType). If you haven't done so already, read the previous chapter and organize your fonts.

In general, the font management utilities work like this:

Instead of opening or closing fonts by moving them into and out of the System folder, open or close them through the font management utility.

Create sets, or lists, of the fonts that you use in certain projects. When you decide to work in a specific project, open the utility and from there open the set that contains the necessary fonts. You can add to or delete from a set at any time. You can close one set and open another. You can open more than one set at a time, even if they contain the same font names in their lists.

Open and close fonts while you are in the middle of a project. Many applications (especially the newest versions) allow you to open a font while you are working—voilà, it appears in your menu. Some applications make you quit and re-open (darn it) before the font will appear in the menu.

All of these utilities also allow you to share fonts over a network, but keep in mind that sharing fonts over a network is dreadfully slow, and you need multi-user font licenses. Read the manual for specific instructions on sharing fonts over a network.

Manage your fonts with Adobe Type Manager Deluxe

The Deluxe version of ATM started with version 4.0, so if you have any version of ATM before 4.0, you definitely do not have the version that includes font management. It is possible to have a "light" version of ATM 4.0 (it's not called "Deluxe") that also does not have font management capabilities. If you see the screen shown below when you open ATM, either from the control panel itself or from the Apple Menu, you have the Deluxe version:

This Deluxe version not only helps you manage your fonts, it does all the rasterizing that ATM has always done to make the type look beautiful on your screen. If you're used to using ATM and are wondering where those controls are that let you allocate more memory, turn it on and off, etc., check the Preferences under the Edit menu (shown on pages 74–75, as well as 34–36).

There are some nice **keyboard shortcuts** you can use in ATM. While ATM is open, go to the Help menu and choose "Keyboard Shortcuts."

	Keyboard Shortcuts
Activation Legend	
✓	Active set or suitcase
•	Inactive set or suitcase
·	Partially active set (at least one suitcase is inactive)
✱	System suitcase (cannot be deactivated)
⊿	Autoactivated suitcase, either by application or global

Keyboard Shortcuts

⌘ I	Activates currently selected set(s) or suitcase(s)
⌘ D	Deactivates currently selected set(s) or suitcase(s)
⌘ Control D	Deactivates suitcase(s) globally
⌘ Option D	Deactivates without prompt
⌘ click on suitcase name	Displays suitcase location (while the mouse is down)
⌘ =	Brings up the Add Suitcases dialog box
⌘ N	Creates a new set
Clear, delete	Deletes selected text, set(s) or suitcase(s)
⌘ Control drag to 🗑	Deletes selected suitcase(s) globally
⌘ Control Clear, delete	Deletes selected suitcase(s) globally
⌘ O	Opens the currently selected set(s) to show a Set window
⌘ option W	Closes all windows except for the main window
⌘ E	Verifies currently selected set(s), suitcase(s) or font(s)
⌘ R	Reports on currently selected set(s), suitcase(s) or font(s)
⌘ F	Brings up the Find Suitcase dialog
⌘ G	Finds the next suitcase/font matching the current Find settings
F5	Selects the Sets Tab
F6	Selects the Fonts Tab
F7	Selects the Set & Fonts Tab
F9	Selects the Known Fonts pop-up menu item
F10	Selects the Active Fonts pop-up menu item
F11	Selects the System Fonts pop-up menu item
F12	Selects the Damaged Fonts pop-up menu item

If you see a hyphen in the keyboard shortcut, like this: ⌘–**D**, don't type the hyphen! I wish they wouldn't write keyboard shortcuts that way. As with any keyboard shortcut on the Mac, hold down the modifier key or keys (like Command, Shift, Option, and/or Control), then *tap* the letter key *once*. With an Fkey shortcut (like F12), just *tap* the Fkey *once*.

Using the ATM Deluxe windows

Below is the window you'll probably work in the most, the Sets & Fonts window. It's just a combination of the individual windows, Sets and Fonts, so everything you see in this illustration applies to either of those other windows.

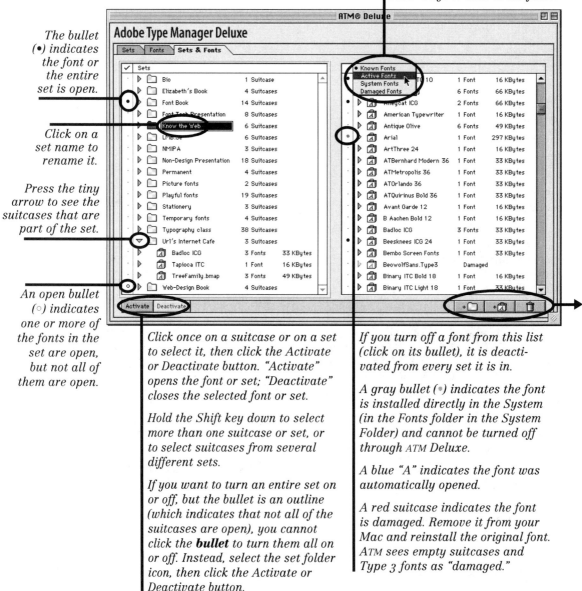

Press on this label to get the menu of other options, which are other ways to look at the fonts.

The bullet (•) indicates the font or the entire set is open.

Click on a set name to rename it.

Press the tiny arrow to see the suitcases that are part of the set.

An open bullet (○) indicates one or more of the fonts in the set are open, but not all of them are open.

Click once on a suitcase or on a set to select it, then click the Activate or Deactivate button. "Activate" opens the font or set; "Deactivate" closes the selected font or set.

Hold the Shift key down to select more than one suitcase or set, or to select suitcases from several different sets.

*If you want to turn an entire set on or off, but the bullet is an outline (which indicates that not all of the suitcases are open), you cannot click the **bullet** to turn them all on or off. Instead, select the set folder icon, then click the Activate or Deactivate button.*

If you turn off a font from this list (click on its bullet), it is deactivated from every set it is in.

A gray bullet (•) indicates the font is installed directly in the System (in the Fonts folder in the System Folder) and cannot be turned off through ATM Deluxe.

A blue "A" indicates the font was automatically opened.

A red suitcase indicates the font is damaged. Remove it from your Mac and reinstall the original font. ATM sees empty suitcases and Type 3 fonts as "damaged."

Drag-and-drop

You can drag-and-drop suitcases from wherever you store your fonts, including a removable hard disk, to open them or to make new sets. You can drag a suitcase into an existing set, or you can drop it directly into the Sets window to add the suitcase without putting it into any set.

Quick tip: Drag a suitcase onto the Sets icon (the little folder icon on the bottom right of the ATM Deluxe window). ATM will make a new, untitled set that you can name, and the fonts you dropped on the icon will already be installed inside. Try it.

Sets and fonts

To make a new set: Click on the folder icon (called the Sets icon) on the bottom right of the window, then name the set. Then click on the suitcase icon. You'll get a standard dialog box; find and double-click any suitcase or individual font that you want to add to the selected set.

To CLOSE a font from one set or to delete an entire set: Select the font or set from the list on the *left* (or from the Sets window), then click the trash icon.

To CLOSE a font from every set it is in: Select the font from the list on the *right* (or from the Fonts window), then click the "Deactivate" button.

To DELETE a font from one set or to delete an entire set: Select the font or set from the list on the *left* (or from the Sets window), then click the trash icon.

To DELETE a font from every set: Select the font from the list on the *right* (or from the Fonts window), then click the trash icon.

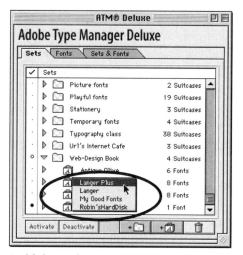

*Hold down the Command key and press on the **name** of any suitcase to see where it is located. For instance, in this example you can see that the Langer Plus suitcase is in a folder called Langer, which is in a folder called My Good Fonts, which is on my hard disk.*

Other tips

Double-click any *set* to get a window that displays the contents.

Double-click any *suitcase* to display what the typeface looks like. Experiment with the buttons in that window.

Use the Tools menu to alphabetize (Sort) the contents of the windows, to check for damaged fonts (Verify), and to see a report of the font information (Report).

Use the File menu to print a sample of the typeface and its information. It will print the sample text you enter in the Preferences (see page 75), plus examples in several sizes.

Also use the File menu to print a font index, which is one line of each face in the suitcase or set.

Read the manual.

ATM Deluxe Preferences (from the File menu)

If you're going to use ATM Deluxe, you might as well know what to do with all the Preferences settings. I'll go over the basic and most important features here, but you really should read your manual and the ReadMe file for all the details.

From the File menu, choose "Preferences...." If "General" isn't chosen from the little menu at the top left (as shown), choose it.

The **Character Cache Size** lets you allocate more of your memory (RAM) to ATM to allow it to display characters on the screen. If you use a lot of fonts in one publication, if you use Multiple Masters, or if you set type in very large sizes, you will probably want to add more memory here. Add about 50K per individual font that you have open. You'll need to restart for it to take effect.

When you set type in Photoshop, do the top or bottom edges of the characters get cut off? Come to the General Preferences and choose "Character shapes" under the **Preserve** section. When you set type in Microsoft Word, do you get odd line spacing when you type superscripts or subscripts? Choose "Line spacing." The default is "Line spacing" and it should generally stay there unless you have the character shape problem in Photoshop or other graphic program.

Precision Character Positioning lets ATM use its own grid to position characters very precisely on the page, *if* the application supports "fractional widths." PageMaker and Quark automatically use fractional width spacing, but you will have to turn it on in Microsoft Word (use Page Setup) or Claris-Works (use Preferences) before you turn on Precision Character Positioning in ATM.

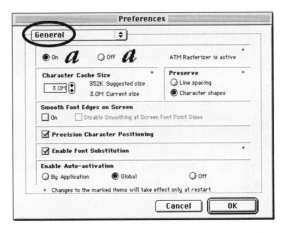

If you choose **Smooth Font Edges on Screen,** ATM will "anti-alias" the edges of the type, but only while they are displayed on the screen (meaning they won't print that way). To anti-alias, ATM blends the color of the type with the color of the background, as you can see if you look closely at the examples below. On large type this can look very nice (on the screen), but it gives a soft, fuzzy look to small type. And depending on the colors you have available on your monitor, type on a colored background can appear with a "halo" (icky stuff) around the edges. This really becomes a problem on web pages. If the type on web pages has halos, turn this feature off. You don't need to restart.

Smoothing on ➡
(anti-aliasing on).

◀ *Smoothing off*
(no anti-aliasing).

Choose **Enable Font Substitution** if you want ATM to try to emulate a font you don't have if it appears in a document. ATM can only emulate fonts whose names it finds in its database (which is stored in the System Folder). If you have trouble printing in programs like ClarisWorks or Acrobat, disable font substitution and restart.

ATM can automatically open the fonts in a document as you open the document, *if* you have turned on the **Enable Auto-activation** feature.

 If you choose "By Application," the fonts that were opened automatically will be closed when you close the application. You can't close these auto-activated fonts yourself; they won't close until you quit the application.

 If you choose "Global," the font remains open until you turn off your Mac.

 To use auto-activation with PageMaker, go to the General Preferences, click the "Map fonts…" button, and choose "ATM font matching."

You should read the ReadMe file for more information about this feature.

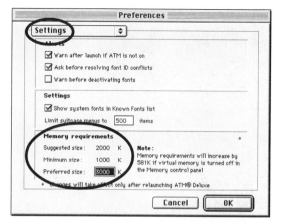

The important part of the "Settings" Preferences is the **Memory requirements.** If you use ATM a lot and have lots of sets, move things in and out, or open and close fonts and sets, then allocate more RAM here. ATM will only use this RAM when it's open, whereas the Character Cache you set in the General Preferences is taken by ATM all the time.

Play around with your choices in the "Printing" Preferences. Retype the "Sampler text" to whatever you want to see when you choose to "Print Sample…" from the File menu. Press the "Sampler text" menu to see what other options you have in printing font samples.

Manage your fonts with Suitcase

Suitcase 3.0

What is Suitcase?

Suitcase is a font management utility, now from Symantec Corporation. It used to be the best one available, but version 3.0 removed several of the previous version's best features, so I can't say it's the best anymore. Don't confuse the name Suitcase (with a capital S, the utility from Symantec) with the *suitcase icons* that store fonts (with a lowercase s, from Apple). Although it is the same word, they really have nothing to do with each other. *Just because you have icons of suitcases does not mean in any way that you have the utility Suitcase.*

In this section I'm going to give you a run-down on how to use Suitcase, but I highly recommend you actually **read** the Suitcase manual.

Versions of Suitcase

I actually prefer the previous version of Suitcase, version 2.1.4. If you have version 3.0, make sure you go to the Symantec web site (www.symantec.com) and download the upgrade to bring your version up to at least version 3.0.1, which fixes a couple of small but troublesome features.

To find out exactly which version you have, click once on the application icon, then press Command I (or choose "Get Info" from the File menu). The Get Info window will tell you which version you're using.

Suitcase 3.0

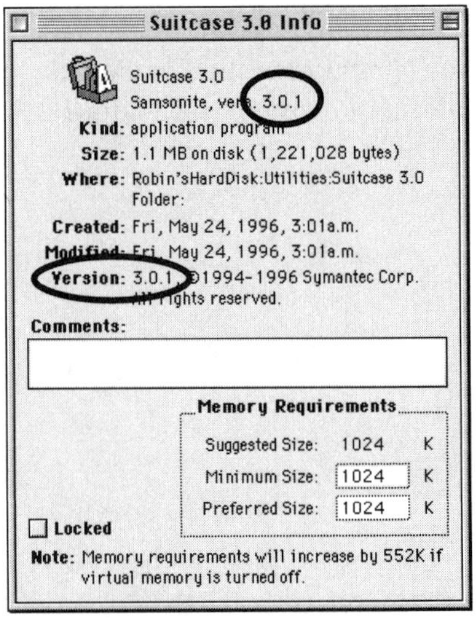

	Suitcase 3.0 Info	
	Suitcase 3.0 Samsonite, ver. 3.0.1	

Kind: application program
Size: 1.1 MB on disk (1,221,028 bytes)
Where: Robin'sHardDisk:Utilities:Suitcase 3.0 Folder:

Created: Fri, May 24, 1996, 3:01a.m.
Modified: Fri, May 24, 1996, 3:01a.m.
Version: 3.0.1, ©1994–1996 Symantec Corp. All rights reserved.

Comments:

Memory Requirements
Suggested Size: 1024   K
Minimum Size: 1024   K
Preferred Size: 1024   K

☐ **Locked**

Note: Memory requirements will increase by 552K if virtual memory is turned off.

Suitcase, the old version (up to 2.1.4)   Suitcase™ 2.1.4

Below is the dialog box from Suitcase version 2.1.4. The newer version, 3.0, is completely different from this version, but just in case you have the older one (which still works with Mac OS 8, and which I prefer over the newer one), here is a quick sampling of how to use it. The rest of this chapter is about Suitcase 3.0.

*This is the list of **sets.** The ones you see here come with Suitcase. You can make lots of others.*

*All fonts in the **Permanent** set will automatically open when you turn on your Mac.*

*All fonts in the **Temporary** set (or in any set you create) will close when you shut down.*

Double-click one or more of your sets to have that set(s) open at startup. *Its name will be in italic. When you no longer want that set to open at startup, double-click its name again so it is not italic.**

*****Opened Suitcases*** *shows you all suitcases in all sets that are currently open. Opened suitcases are underlined. **You can close any font from here.****

*****Closed Suitcases*** *lists all the fonts that have ever been open. It is sometimes faster to open or add suitcases from this list than to navigate to your fonts folder.**

*When you cut or copy suitcase names from the set list, they do not go to the regular Macintosh Clipboard; they go to a special **Suitcase Clipboard.** Just as with the regular Clipboard, this Clipboard holds only one group of selected items at a time. You can check here to see what is currently being held in it.*

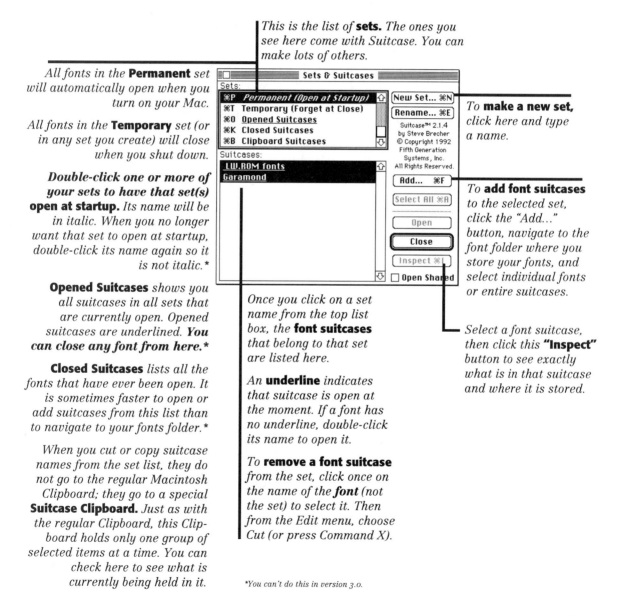

*To **make a new set,** click here and type a name.*

*To **add font suitcases** to the selected set, click the "Add..." button, navigate to the font folder where you store your fonts, and select individual fonts or entire suitcases.*

*Select a font suitcase, then click this **"Inspect"** button to see exactly what is in that suitcase and where it is stored.*

*Once you click on a set name from the top list box, the **font suitcases** that belong to that set are listed here.*

*An **underline** indicates that suitcase is open at the moment. If a font has no underline, double-click its name to open it.*

*To **remove a font suitcase** from the set, click once on the name of the **font** (not the set) to select it. Then from the Edit menu, choose Cut (or press Command X).*

*You can't do this in version 3.0.

Opening Suitcase

Open Suitcase

You installed Suitcase and restarted, right?
You can open Suitcase by going to the Apple
menu and choosing "Suitcase."

Or use the hot key (Command Option S)—
just press those keys and Suitcase will open,
even if you're in an application. In some
applications, however, this hot key may
conflict with another key combination.
If you don't want Suitcase to use that hot
key: Open Suitcase, choose "Preferences...'
from the Edit menu, and uncheck the box,
"Hot-Key to open Suitcase application."

Can't find Suitcase?

If you closed the Suitcase window but did
not actually quit, then when you open
Suitcase again, nothing seems to appear.
Watch the menu bar, though—it changes
when Suitcase is active. When you see the
menu bar as shown below, go to the View
menu and choose "Show Sets," or press
Command 1. Yes, this can be really irritating.

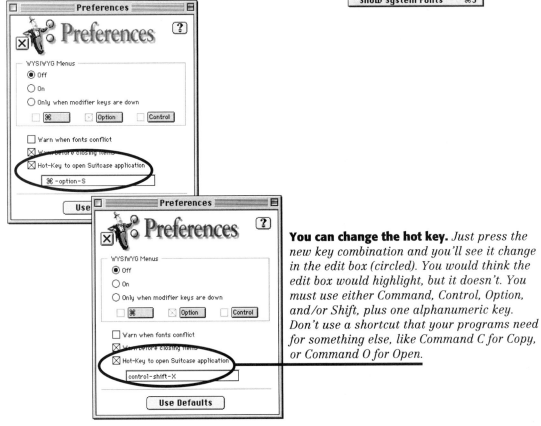

You can change the hot key. *Just press the
new key combination and you'll see it change
in the edit box (circled). You would think the
edit box would highlight, but it doesn't. You
must use either Command, Control, Option,
and/or Shift, plus one alphanumeric key.
Don't use a shortcut that your programs need
for something else, like Command C for Copy,
or Command O for Open.*

Creating and using sets

Sets

To open fonts in Suitcase, you must first create a set and then put your fonts into that set (or into any other existing set).

First you should decide which fonts you want open all the time and put those into the **Startup Set** which Suitcase has already made for you. When you restart (or crash and reboot), the fonts in the Startup Set will open automatically, and the fonts in every other set you make will not, which is very annoying. In the previous version of Suitcase, you could choose any number of sets to open on startup, but in this version you have only this one Startup Set.

To create a set, click on the "New Set…" button. This puts a new suitcase icon in the Sets window, and it's waiting for you to name it (as shown on the following page). Name the set with a name that gives you a clue what the set is for.

Click the "Add…" button. Navigate to the folder where you store all your fonts (as shown on the following page), and open the suitcases you want in this set. Click "Done" when you've added what you need.

To open a set, double-click on its name.

To open a font without putting it into a set, see page 81.

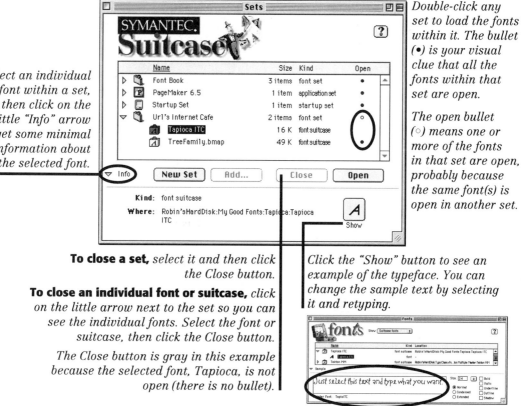

Select an individual font within a set, then click on the little "Info" arrow to get some minimal information about the selected font.

Double-click any set to load the fonts within it. The bullet (•) is your visual clue that all the fonts within that set are open.

The open bullet (○) means one or more of the fonts in that set are open, probably because the same font(s) is open in another set.

To close a set, *select it and then click the Close button.*

To close an individual font or suitcase, *click on the little arrow next to the set so you can see the individual fonts. Select the font or suitcase, then click the Close button.*

The Close button is gray in this example because the selected font, Tapioca, is not open (there is no bullet).

Click the "Show" button to see an example of the typeface. You can change the sample text by selecting it and retyping.

More about making sets

Make a new set

When you click the "New Set" button, a new suitcase icon appears, waiting for you to name it, as shown below. Give it a name.

Give the set a name that will provide a good clue as to what the set contains or what it's for.

Add fonts to the set

To add fonts to the selected set, click the "Add…" button. You get a standard sort of Open dialog box (shown below). Find your fonts folder ("My Good Fonts") just like you find any folder on your Mac. Double-click on the name of the folder in which you stored the font you want. Select the individual font or the suitcase, then click "Add."

When you open a family folder, the names of all the suitcases stored in that folder will appear. You can open any or all of them.

If your fonts are not in a suitcase, as shown in the example below, each screen font or each TrueType font will be displayed.

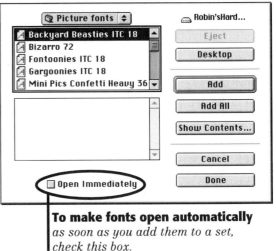

To make fonts open automatically *as soon as you add them to a set, check this box.*

(Unfortunately, Suitcase gives you no clue in this dialog box as to the name of the set you are adding fonts into, nor which fonts are already in the set.)

Open a font without putting it into a set

Sometimes you just want to open a couple of fonts to play with. From the File menu choose "Add to Temporary…." Any font you add this way will close when you shutdown or crash and will not be listed in any set.

If you want to see which fonts are temporarily opened, choose "Show Temporary Fonts" from the View menu, or press Command 3.

To close a font you added temporarily, view the temporary fonts (as described above). Click once on the font you want to close, then from the Edit menu, choose "Remove Selected Items…."

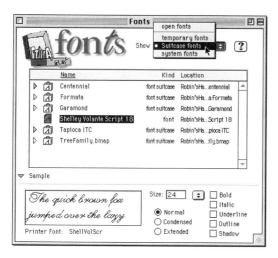

Delete an entire set

If you want to delete an entire set, just select the set (click once on its icon). Then from the Edit menu, choose "Remove Selected Items…."

Or you can select the set and simply hit the Delete key. You'll get a dialog box asking if you really want to remove it.

Close a font or suitcase in a set

If you just want to *close* a font or suitcase in a set, select the font or suitcase within the set, then click the "Close" button. This just closes the font, but does not remove it from the set.

Delete a font or suitcase from a set

To permanently *delete* a font or suitcase from a set, open the set (click its little triangle) and select the font or suitcase (click once on its icon). Then from the Edit menu, choose "Remove Selected Items…."

Or you can select the font or suitcase and hit the Delete key. You'll get a dialog box asking if you really want to remove it.

It would be nice if you could, as in version 2.1.4, delete or close a font from the "Open Fonts" window. But you can't. You have to know exactly which set contains the font you want to delete, which can be a pain in the wazoo if you have lots of sets.

For more help with Suitcase

Use the Help menu

Check out the Help menu in Suitcase. You can get most of your questions answered here, and it can be easier than using the manual. You can either use the Help menu (shown below), or click on the question mark icon in any of the Suitcase windows (shown below) to go straight to the full Guide.

To use any of the Suitcase Help features, you must have AppleGuide running on your Mac. Unless you have physically turned AppleGuide off in the Extensions Manager, it should be running.

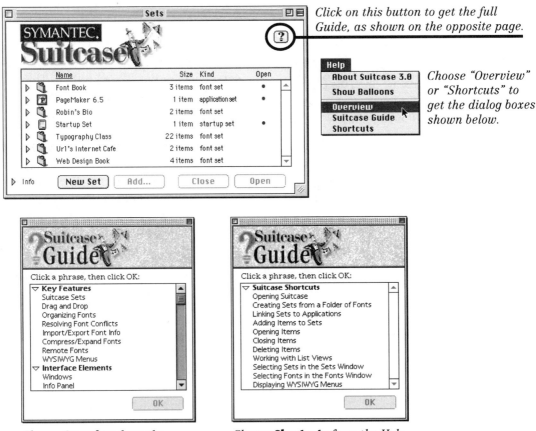

Click on this button to get the full Guide, as shown on the opposite page.

Choose "Overview" or "Shortcuts" to get the dialog boxes shown below.

*Choose **Overview** from the Help menu to get this window. Double-click on any phrase to get more information about it.*

*Choose **Shortcuts** from the Help menu to get this window. Double-click on any phrase to get information and shortcut tips about it.*

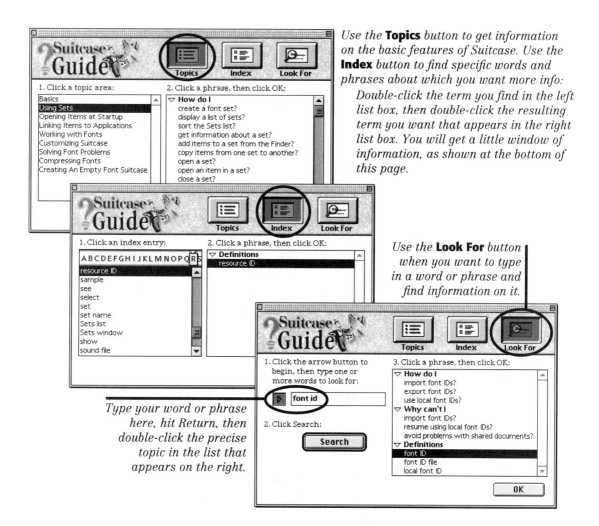

Use the **Topics** *button to get information on the basic features of Suitcase. Use the* **Index** *button to find specific words and phrases about which you want more info:*

Double-click the term you find in the left list box, then double-click the resulting term you want that appears in the right list box. You will get a little window of information, as shown at the bottom of this page.

Use the **Look For** *button when you want to type in a word or phrase and find information on it.*

Type your word or phrase here, hit Return, then double-click the precise topic in the list that appears on the right.

When you finally double-click any term in any of these help features, you will get a little window like this:

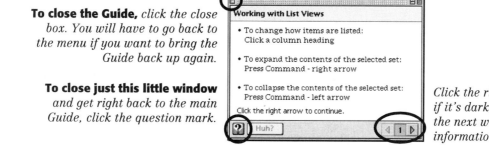

To close the Guide, *click the close box. You will have to go back to the menu if you want to bring the Guide back up again.*

To close just this little window *and get right back to the main Guide, click the question mark.*

Click the right arrow, if it's dark, to go to the next window of information.

Create a Font ID file

Font identification (ID) problems are not as prevalent as they used to be, thanks to better technology. It is rare now for a font to get confused about itself, like Bodoni thinking it is Palatino. Much of the confusion is solved by these font management programs.

But if you take your document to another computer, perhaps to your office or to a service bureau, and discover that fonts are confused about who they are, you might want to make a "Font ID file" and use it.

The Font ID file contains all the identification numbers that your Mac uses to identify your fonts. Depending on whether your application calls on fonts by name or by number, the other computer may look at

those identification numbers and apply a different font, one that matches the font ID number of a font within their system. (Microsoft Word is one of the few applications that still calls on fonts by number; most others use the name.)

So you create this ID file and take it with your fonts to your service bureau. They open Suitcase and choose the menu item you see below, "Export Font IDs...." They open your font ID file and everything works fine.

When they are done running your job, it is very important that they go back into the Suitcase menu and choose "Use Local Font IDs" so their computer gets back to normal.

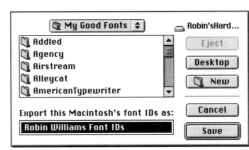

Open Suitcase, and from the Tools menu, choose "Export Font IDs...."

Save the file with a name you will remember and in a place where you will find it.

Robin Williams Font IDs

Take this file to your service bureau, if necessary. You may have to tell them how to use it. This file is only useful if the other computer also uses Suitcase.

Manage your fonts with MasterJuggler

MasterJuggler™

MasterJuggler

MasterJuggler is another excellent utility that allows you to store hundreds of fonts outside of your System Folder (where they don't take up RAM and where you have no limit to the number of fonts available), and then open just the fonts you need for the project you are working on.

In this section I'm going to give you a rundown on how to use MasterJuggler, but the manual is pretty good. I highly recommend you actually **read** the manual. But then, if you read the manual, you probably wouldn't need to read this book.

Your fonts should be organized before you use any font management utility. They can either be all in one giant folder, or, as I recommended in the previous chapter, you can store each family in a separate folder that contains both the suitcase and the printer fonts (unless they are TrueType). If you haven't done so already, read the section beginning on page 69 and organize your fonts.

What you can do in MasterJuggler

You can choose to have just the fonts you need open when you need them. The fonts that you open will stay open until you manually close them, and they will re-open when you restart your Mac.

You can choose to "temporarily" open an individual font, a suitcase, or an entire set. When you shut down, those temporary fonts are forgotten and will not open automatically the next time you turn on your Mac.

You can open and close fonts while you are in the middle of a project. Most current page layout and graphics applications will allow you to open a font while you are working—voilà, it appears in your menu. Some applications make you quit and re-open (darn it) before the font appears. And some applications will crash if you change fonts midstream. You just have to check it out. (In Photoshop 4, you can force the font menu to update: select the Type tool, then hold down the Shift key and click on the page.)

MasterJuggler menu

The MasterJuggler menu

MasterJuggler lets you access its menu in several ways. Because this program does much more than manage fonts, you'll see other things in its menu (you'll need to read the manual to find out how to use the other features, because that's not the point of this book). The only items in the menu you need to worry about right now are MasterJuggler, Font List, and FontShow.

After you install MasterJuggler, it will appear in your Apple menu, as shown above.

If you hold down the Shift key while you press on the Apple menu, your Apple menu will disappear and all you'll see is your MasterJuggler menu.

*If you set a **hot key,** the MasterJuggler menu will appear wherever you click on your screen while holding down the hot key combination (see page 92). Sometimes it appears when you don't want it.*

Making sets

Sets in MasterJuggler

One of the most effective ways to use MasterJuggler is to make sets of fonts, then open or close those entire sets with one click. You can, of course, open individual fonts or suitcases (details on the next page), but you'll find that the set features are what makes font management utilities so useful.

When you add a font to a set, you are just adding the *name* of the font to the set—you're not actually putting the font itself anywhere. This means you can add the same font or suitcase to any number of sets.

You can create sets within sets. For instance, in the example on the opposite page I made several sets of script faces, categorized by "personalities" (casual, formal, or fun). Thus I have three individual sets, but I then made one more set called "Scripts," and into it I added the three individual script sets. You never know when this might be useful.

It's very easy to make a set. See the directions on the opposite page. Make them anytime, even in the middle of a project, and add to a set or delete from it at anytime.

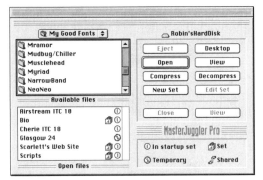

*This is a list of sets in MasterJuggler. This is the **main window** you will work with.*

Before you start to make sets, you should **make a new folder** in which to store your collection of sets (**❶**). MasterJuggler creates a new file for each set, and you need to tell it where to store that new file.

To make a new set:
- Open MasterJuggler.
- Click the "New Set" button.
- Name the new set (**❷**) and save it into the new folder you made.
- Find the folder where you store all of your fonts (**❸**) and add individual fonts, entire suitcases, or other sets to this set by double-clicking the font file.
- Click "Done."

To add or delete a file to an existing set:
- Open MasterJuggler.
- If the set you want to edit (add or delete a file from) is open, close it. You can double-click the set to close it.
- In the upper list of the main window, select the set name, then click the "Edit Set" button. From the new window you can add or delete font files.

To close (not delete) an individual file in an open set:
- See the caption on page 89.

To change the name of a set:
- Open the folder in which you store your sets. (If you can't remember where you stored the set, see page 89.)
- Select the set file and change its name just like you change the name of any file on your Mac (click on its name, then type).

MasterJuggler Sets

❶ *I created a new folder in my fonts folder. I put a blank space in front of its name so it would always appear at the top of the list.*

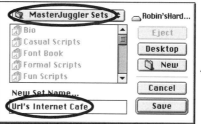

❷ *Name the set and save it into your new folder for sets.*

❸ *Select and add individual fonts, entire suitcases, or other sets to this set.*

Url's Internet Cafe

After you make a set, you will see a file on your hard drive that looks like this—an icon of a couple of suitcases instead of just one.

Opening and closing font files

Open fonts or sets "permanently"

In the top half of the MasterJuggler dialog box (shown below), navigate to and open the font files you need; just select them and click "Open," or double-click their names. The open files will be displayed in the bottom half of the window. Fonts in the "startup set" are considered to be "permanent" because *they automatically reopen when you restart your Mac,* **unless** *you open them "temporarily."*

Open fonts or sets "temporarily"

In the Options dialog box (press Command T to get it), there is an option that says, "All new file opens are temp." If you put a checkmark in this box, every font you open will be considered "temporary" and will close when you shut down your computer or when you crash. This checkbox default is off, which means your fonts will *not* be temporary when you open them. You can, of course, check it so every font you open is temporary.

However, generally you *want* fonts to remain open permanently, and *sometimes* you want them to be temporary. So you can **override the default:** hold the Command key down when you open the font suitcase. This will cause that one font to load temporarily.

But, if you did check the option box to make all new files open temporarily, then when you hold down the Command key it will do just the opposite—it will open the font permanently. Remember, the Command key *overrides* the setting in the checkbox.

Close fonts or sets

In the bottom list box, double-click any font, suitcase, or set you want to close. Remember, opening and closing fonts can cause problems in some applications. If your fonts don't work quite right after you open or close them through MasterJuggler, quit the application you're working in and reopen it.

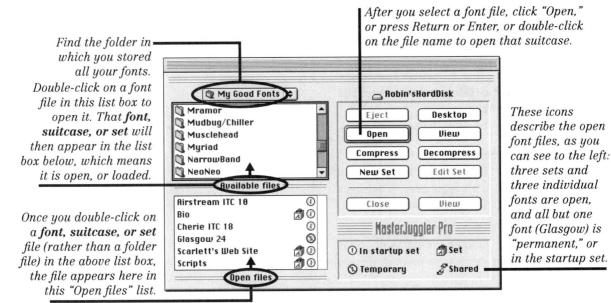

Find the folder in which you stored all your fonts. Double-click on a font file in this list box to open it. That font, suitcase, or set will then appear in the list box below, which means it is open, or loaded.

Once you double-click on a font, suitcase, or set file (rather than a folder file) in the above list box, the file appears here in this "Open files" list.

After you select a font file, click "Open," or press Return or Enter, or double-click on the file name to open that suitcase.

These icons describe the open font files, as you can see to the left: three sets and three individual fonts are open, and all but one font (Glasgow) is "permanent," or in the startup set.

Hold down the Option key and press on the name of an open font file. You will get this little menu that tells you where the font is stored. The hierarchy is gray because you can't choose any of those items—it is just the path that tells you where the file is stored.

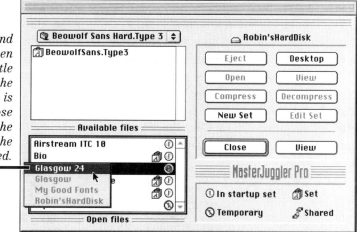

In the Options dialog box (press Command T), there is an option to "Show all open files in open list." If you check that box, Master-Juggler will not only list the set names, but will list each individual font within each set. These set fonts appear in italic, as shown to the right. Option-click on any of the italic names to get a list of where the set it stored, plus the name of the set the font is within.

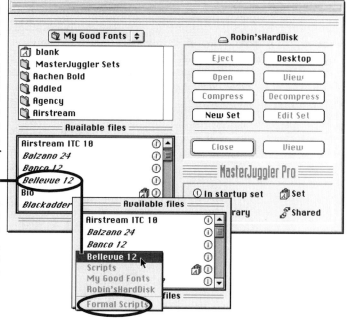

To close just one font in a set,
go to the Options dialog box (Command T), and choose "Show all open files in open list." Then in the main window you can select the individual font (it will be italic) and **close** *it (double-click its name). This does not* **delete** *the file from the set! (To delete a font file from a set, use the Edit button.)*

Viewing fonts in MasterJuggler

View fonts

If you don't know what a typeface looks like, you can view any font even before you open it. Just select a font suitcase in either the top or bottom list, then click the View button on the top (Command V) or bottom (Command 2). That gives you the little dialog box shown below. Click the "Font faces" radio button to see the actual faces.

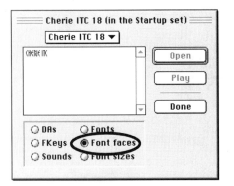

Unfortunately, the font face only appears in about 10 point, no matter what size you have installed. For a better view of the font, see FontShow (opposite page).

Font List

From the MasterJuggler menu, choose "Font List" to see all of the open fonts in their typefaces, as shown below.

This is an example of the Font List. The Help dialog box below shows you all the keyboard shortcuts you can use to display this list in various ways.

Press Command T to gray out all fonts except the bitmaps (QuickDraw fonts, as MasterJuggler calls them). Press Command T again to gray out all except PostScript fonts.

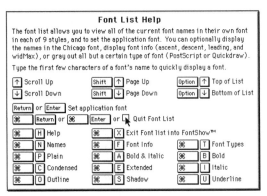

Click the little question mark in the upper-right corner of the Font List to get this Help dialog box.

FontShow

From the MasterJuggler menu, choose "FontShow." You can see the open fonts in a variety of sizes, styles, sample text, etc. Experiment with the buttons!

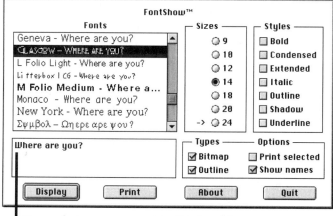

Type whatever you want in this box, then click the "Display" button to see that text in each of your open fonts.

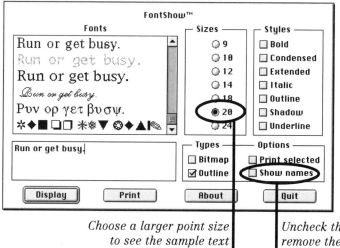

The second example (in the list to the left) is gray because the "Bitmap" button is unchecked under "Types," and that font is a bitmap.

Choose a larger point size to see the sample text displayed in that size.

Uncheck the "Show names" checkbox to remove the font names from the list. You will still see the sample text displayed.

Making and using Hot Keys

Hot Keys

A "hot key" is a keyboard combination that makes things happen without having to go to any menu. You can set a number of hot keys within MasterJuggler. You can make the application open; make the menu appear anywhere on the screen; display a list of fonts that are loaded in your Mac, and see them in their typeface (Font list); display a more powerful list of the fonts that are loaded (FontShow); and once you know how to use the other features of MasterJuggler, you can make those other features appear with the tap of a keyboard combination.

Would you like to see a list of your open fonts like this appear with the click of a key? Set a hot key (next page) for "Font list." When I press Command F9, this list appears in front of me. The current default font is highlighted.

To create Hot Keys, open MasterJuggler by choosing it from the Apple menu.

- Press Command T, or choose "Options…" from the Special menu.

- The first edit box ("MJ Appl," which stands for MasterJuggler Application) is selected for you. You just type the keyboard shortcut you want to use as the hot key, and MasterJuggler will enter it into this selected edit box. *This keyboard combination will make the MasterJuggler application open and its window appear.* Here, I have set **Command `** (same as the tilde key, ~) as the hot key (MasterJuggler adds the useless hyphen in the middle of the keyboard shortcut; ignore it).

- Tab down to select "Font list" and type a hot key, then tab down to "FontShow" and type a hot key. See pages 90 and 91 for what these useful items are.

- You can create a hot key *that will display the MasterJuggler menu anywhere on the screen* by holding down those keys and clicking the mouse button anywhere except on the menu bar. (If you're not using Mac OS 8, you'll have to hold the mouse button down to see the Master-Juggler menu.)

To set the hot key, tab on down to the space for "MJ pop-up." MasterJuggler won't let you choose just any key combination for this hot key. Once you have selected the box, press the Enter key to cycle through your options; the options will appear in the box. When you decide on the keystrokes you want to use, hit Tab to move to another box, or hit Return to accept the choice and close this Options window.

```
╔═══════════════════════════ Options ═══════════════════════════╗
║  ┌─ Hot Keys ─────────────────┐  ┌─ General Options ──────────┐ ║
║  │ MJ Appl    [⌘ - `        ]  │  │ ☑ Engage Font Guardian™... │ ║
║  │ Appl list  [            ]  │  │ ☑ Resolve font number conflicts │
║  │ DA list    [            ]  │  │ ☐ Warn on unresolved conflicts │
║  │ Font list  [⌘ - f 9      ]  │  │ ☐ All new file opens are shared │
║  │ FKey list  [            ]  │  │ ☐ All new file opens are temp │
║  │ Sound list [            ]  │  │ ☐ Show all open files in open list │
║  │ FontShow   [⌘ - f 10     ]  │  │ ☐ Warn on font file close │
║  │ HotSounds  [            ]  │  │ ☐ Skip unfound files at startup │
║  │ KeyChains  [            ]  │  │ ☐ Wait for all disks to mount │
║  │ ResConflicts[           ]  │  │ ☑ Quick sort font menus │
║  │ Bypass     [Shift        ]  │  │ ☐ Remember current default dir │
║  │ MJ pop-up  [⌘-shift-control-click]│ ☑ Show documents in pop-up │
║  │ Appl pop-up[Inactive     ]  │                              │
║  │ Wnd pop-up [Inactive     ]  │  ( Cancel )  ( Save )         │
║  └────────────────────────────┘  └────────────────────────────┘ ║
╚════════════════════════════════════════════════════════════════╝
```

This is the Options dialog box. Experiment with the General Options, or read the manual for full details on each option.

MasterJuggler has some restrictions and specifications on assigning and using these Hot Keys. If you have any trouble or any questions, check the manual!!!

And keep in mind that these hot key shortcuts will overpower any similar keyboard shortcuts in your applications. For instance, the keyboard shortcut to show the Preferences dialog box in PageMaker is Command K. So if I use MasterJuggler's default Command K hot key, it overpowers the PageMaker shortcut and I can no longer get my Preferences dialog box in PageMaker unless I go to the menu. So I changed the MasterJuggler hot key.

Gather fonts for remote viewing or printing

Gather fonts

If you have a set of fonts that you need to send to a service bureau, MasterJuggler will gather the fonts in that set and put copies of them into a new folder, ready for transporting. Now, this does not necessarily mean that every font you used in a project will be contained in that new folder—only the fonts in the set or sets that you select will be in there. It's entirely possible (I know this) to make a set of fonts for a project, then while you're working on the document, you add another font or two onto your page. These other fonts were in your font menu, right? But even though they were in your *font menu,* it doesn't mean they were in that *project set.*

To gather fonts:

- Open MasterJuggler and choose "Gather Fonts…" from the Special menu.

- Use the upper list to choose individual fonts, suitcases, or sets whose fonts you want to gather together (see ❶).

- Click "Done." You'll get the next dialog box, where you can rename the gathered fonts folder and choose a place to store it (see ❷). Make sure the button is checked for "Gather PostScript Outline Files." Click "Gather."

- When MasterJuggler is finished, you'll have a new folder, stored wherever you told it to be stored, named with whatever you named it, and inside are the bitmaps and printer fonts that belong to the set(s) (see ❸).

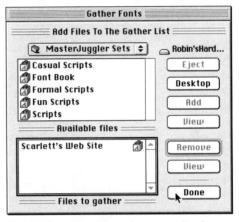

❶ *Add font files from the upper list by double-clicking their names. Click "Done" to get the next dialog box (shown below).*

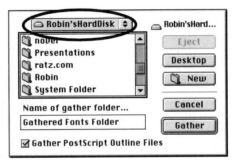

❷ *Choose where you want to store this new folder, and rename it, if you like. The new folder will be stored in whichever folder or disk is displayed at the top of the list box (circled, above).*

Gathered Fonts Folder

❸ *You'll have a folder containing copies of all of the fonts in the selected set.*

Manage your fonts with Font Reserve

Font Reserve

Font Reserve

This is a new and incredibly cool program. Font Reserve truly *manages* your fonts in a completely different way from any other utility. It scans your collection, matches up PostScript pairs, sorts TrueType, checks for corruption problems, solves font identification problems, gets rid of superfluous stuff, makes a database of everything you have, and hides your fonts in an invisible folder called The Vault. (You can choose to make it visible at any time.) You never have to look at or organize your fonts again—Font Reserve will do it for you. You will have a "browser" window from which you open and close fonts, make sets, see what they look like, add more to the collection, and take advantage of other features.

If you're used to working intimately with your fonts, you might find some reluctance at first to letting go and letting Font Reserve take care of them for you, especially since you never again have to work with the physical font files. But it's okay—you still *feel* like you are touching them physically. And you can go look at them anytime you like.

I should've told you . . .

If you're using Font Reserve, you don't have to do a lot of the font cleanup I showed you in Chapter 11—Font Reserve does most of it for you. All you have to do is drop fonts, folders of fonts, or even disks of fonts onto the DropFont icon (shown below) and Font Reserve takes care of everything else. The one thing it doesn't do right now is get rid of superfluous screen sizes, so if you don't want or need the extra bitmaps (the 9, 10, 12, 14, 18, or 24-point fixed-sizes), then you should eliminate them before adding a font to Font Reserve.

Font Reserve Browser

The browser is the main window from which you will work.

Font Reserve Vault

The vault is usually invisible. It stores the fonts in very particular places—don't touch anything in here!

Font Reserve Database

The database keeps track of everything.

DropSet   DropFont

Font Reserve makes aliases of these on your Desktop. Use them to add fonts to the main database or to make new sets.

95

The Font Reserve browser window

The browser window

This is the main interface for Font Reserve. Use this window to make sets, review and preview your fonts, make copies of typefaces, add new ones, etc.

Fonts or sets can be opened "temporarily," which means those fonts will automatically close when you turn off the Mac. If you open a font or set "permanently," it will reopen when you turn your Mac back on.

Click an open bullet (○) to open a font temporarily. A gray bullet (•) means the font is temporarily open (loaded); click on the bullet to close the font.

Select a font and click the "Perm" button above to open a font permanently. And see the shortcut on page 98.

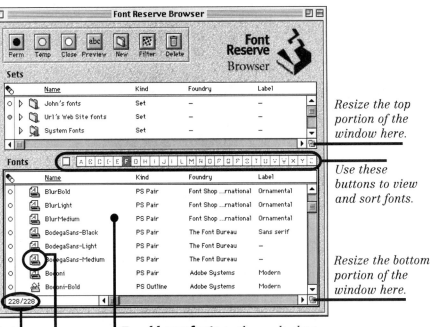

Resize the top portion of the window here.

Use these buttons to view and sort fonts.

Resize the bottom portion of the window here.

This is how many font files are in the vault. If you've done a search (filter), the first number is how many fonts match the search/filter parameters.

These icons tell you what format the font is, and whether it is a healthy PostScript pair or not. See the manual for details about what each icon means.

To add new fonts *to the vault, drag-and-drop them onto this window or onto the icon shown below (which is probably an alias on your Desktop). You can drop an entire folder onto this window or icon, or drop individual fonts or suitcases. Font Reserve will scan them and put either the originals, copies, or aliases (whichever you choose in Preferences) into the vault. From then on, access the fonts from this window.*

DropFont

Experiment

Check out all the various features you find in the menus and in the browser window. This program is very well designed—it won't take you long to find your way around and be in complete control.

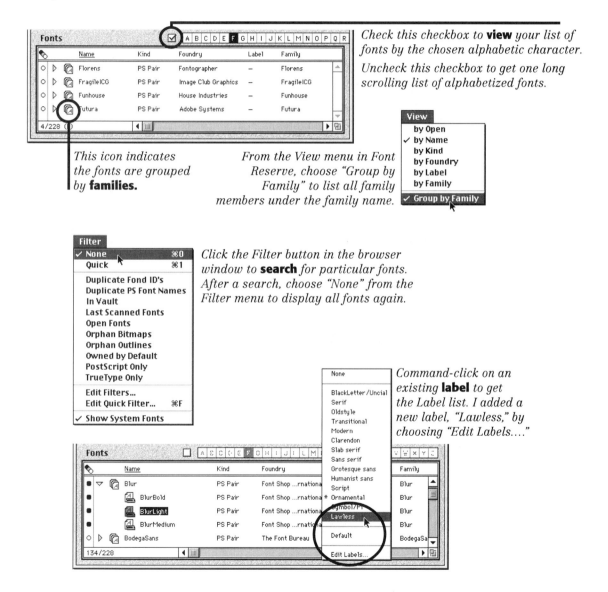

*Check this checkbox to **view** your list of fonts by the chosen alphabetic character.*

Uncheck this checkbox to get one long scrolling list of alphabetized fonts.

*This icon indicates the fonts are grouped by **families.***

From the View menu in Font Reserve, choose "Group by Family" to list all family members under the family name.

*Click the Filter button in the browser window to **search** for particular fonts. After a search, choose "None" from the Filter menu to display all fonts again.*

*Command-click on an existing **label** to get the Label list. I added a new label, "Lawless," by choosing "Edit Labels...."*

And there's more . . .

Try these little tricks

There are a number of little tricks you can do in the browser window. See page 102 for tips on dragging sets or fonts to the Desktop for gathering them up to take to a service bureau, and see page 97 for a shortcut to making and applying labels. And see below.

You can open and close fonts as described on page 96, or you can hold down the Command key and press on the bullet to get this little menu. Choose to open a font or set temporarily or permanently.

Command-click on the icon for any font in the list to see what it looks like. Font Reserve displays the name of the face.

If a font is bitmapped (as shown below), it is either an alias to a disk that is not accessible at the moment, or it is a bitmap only.

Double-click the name of any font to get a more versatile and extensive preview of it. The sample text is determined in the Preferences dialog box (page 100), but you can simply select what's here and retype whatever you want.

Add fonts to the vault

Add fonts

Okay, if you've read the rest of this information about Font Reserve and think you might like to use it, here is how easy it is to add fonts to its database.

DropFont

❶ *Drag fonts, suitcases, folders, or even disk icons onto this alias.*

❶ See the alias of DropFont on your Desktop? Drag your font folder onto that alias and let go. Or you could drag your font folder onto the Font Reserve browser window (the bottom half; if you drag them into the top half, you'll make a huge set of the folder contents).

❷ Font Reserve will display the Preferences dialog box every time you add fonts. Choose one of the options. Press on the tiny question mark to find more information about each option. Basically, this is what I do:

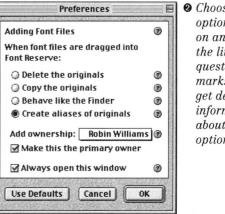

❷ *Choose your option. Click on any of the little question marks to get detailed information about each option.*

If the original font files are on my **hard disk,** I **delete** (move) originals (because I have the real originals from the font vendors on my floppies and CDs).

If the original files are on a **floppy disk,** I drag the entire floppy onto DropFont and choose to **copy** the originals (because I don't want to delete them from the disk).

If the original files are on a **CD,** I drag the selected folders and choose to create **aliases** (because I don't want all those megabytes of fonts on my hard disk). You will have to insert the CD when you want to actually use the font, of course.

❸ *Font Reserve scans the files, adds the fonts to its database, moves the fonts into the vault, and you're done.*

❸ Let Font Reserve do its business, then use the browser window to do yours.

Font Reserve Preferences

Preferences

From the Edit menu, choose "Preferences…" and poke around. Most of it is very self-explanatory, but if you want more info, just press on the tiny question mark you see next to each item. You'll get a great explanation of the feature and when to choose it.

As explained on the previous page, every time you add fonts to Font Reserve, you will automatically get the "Adding Fonts" section of the Preferences dialog box.

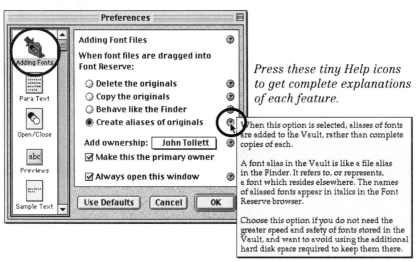

Press these tiny Help icons to get complete explanations of each feature.

So play around with these preferences.

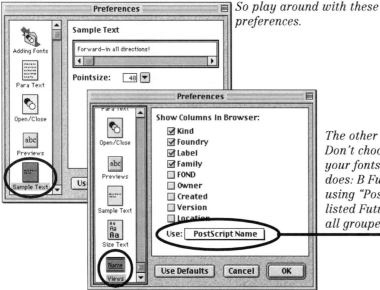

The other option here is "Menu Name." Don't choose that one because it lists your fonts in that silly way your menu does: B Futura Bold, I Futura Italic. By using "PostScript Name," the fonts are listed Futura Bold, Futura Italic, etc., all grouped together in the list.

Preview any font

What does a font look like?

You can preview any font, whether it is actually loaded or not, in a number of different ways. Just double-click on any font in the browser window. The Preview box will appear. Choose an icon on the left that represents what you want to see. Change the type size, the leading (in the "Paragraph" selection), retype the sample text, etc.

If you double-click on a set or on a family icon, you will get an individual preview window for each font in the set or family.

If you have at least version 1.1 of Font Reserve, you can print up specimen sheets of any and all fonts in a variety of different ways, whether they are loaded or not.

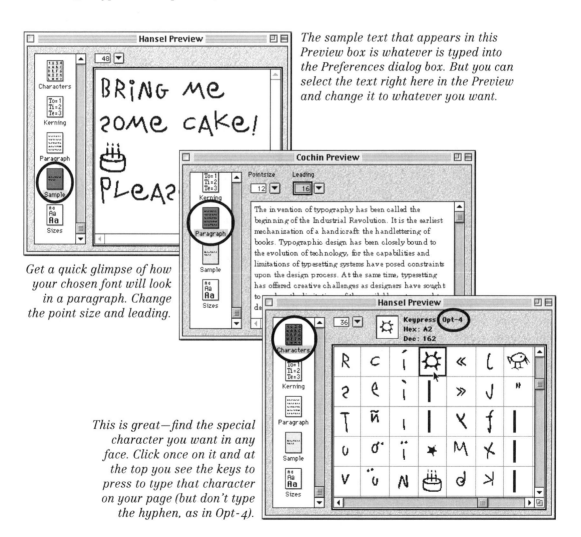

The sample text that appears in this Preview box is whatever is typed into the Preferences dialog box. But you can select the text right here in the Preview and change it to whatever you want.

Get a quick glimpse of how your chosen font will look in a paragraph. Change the point size and leading.

This is great—find the special character you want in any face. Click once on it and at the top you see the keys to press to type that character on your page (but don't type the hyphen, as in Opt-4).

Gather fonts for remote viewing or printing

Gather a set or individual fonts

Sometimes you need to gather up the fonts you used in a project so you can take the file to another computer for printing or even just for viewing. It's so easy in Font Reserve: simply drag the set from the browser window to your Desktop. Font Reserve will make a folder for you, name it the same name as the set, and put copies of all the fonts in the set into that folder.

Don't forget that you may have used a font or two in your document that did not come from the set you made! So don't count on the set to contain every font you need.

You can also drag individual fonts from the lower portion of the window (the Fonts list) or from within any set. It will be easier for you if you make a folder in which to store the fonts first, then drag the individual fonts into that folder.

Font Reserve includes free plug-ins or extensions for QuarkXPress, PageMaker, Illustrator, and several other applications that allow Font Reserve to automatically open all fonts that are in a document, as the document opens, including fonts embedded in EPS graphics. This extension also lets you create a font set with all the fonts used in the document.

Drag a set from the Sets list and drop it onto your Desktop. Font Reserve will make a folder for you, with copies of every font in that set inside the folder, ready for you to take to your service bureau.

Elizabeth's Fonts

102

How to manage your font menu

If your font menu is more than a couple of inches long, you need to fix it. If your font menu shows every individual font listed in some strange order, like B Garamond Bold above I American Typewriter, you need to fix it. If you don't know your typefaces very well, you can have them appear in the menu displaying their faces.

There are several great, inexpensive utilities available for making your font menu manageable. The following pages show you what they look like and point out their best features. You cannot install and use two of these utilites at the same time—they will conflict and cause problems because they are each trying to do the same thing in a different way. You need only **one** of the products in this chapter, not one of each.

```
Arial
Avant Garde
B Garamond Bold
Badloc ICG
Badloc ICG Bevel
Badloc ICG Compression
Bembo
BeoSans-R13
Bermuda Dots
Bermuda Open
Bermuda Solid
Bermuda Squiggle
Bl Garamond BoldItalic
BillsBrackets
BillsDearbornInitials
BillsFatFreddyCaps
BillsFatFreddyExtras
BillsModernDiner
BillsVictorianOrnaments
Blk Centennial Black
Bodoni
Bodoni PosterCompressed
Bookman
C FranklinGothic Condensed
Cancione ITC
Centennial
Centennial BlackItalicOsF
Centennial BlackOsF
Centennial BoldItalicOsF
Centennial BoldOsF
Centennial ItalicOsF
Centennial LightItalicOsF
Centennial LightSC
Centennial RomanSC
Charcoal
CheapMotel
✓ Chicago
Courier
EC FranklinGothic ExtraCond
Eclectic-Regular
Fette Fraktur
Formata Bold
Formata BoldItalic
Formata Italic
Formata Light
▼
```

This is terrible! If your menu looks anything like this, you really need to read this chapter.

TypeTamer

Favorite features: *Most-used fonts are easily accessible; display of typeface samples; easy access of special characters; custom groups of fonts; font can be in more than one group.*

TypeTamer

TypeTamer, from Impossible Software, is a very great tool. On these two pages are examples of what it can do for you. If you don't want to see the special TypeTamer menu, hold down the Shift key before you choose the font menu; you'll get the application's regular font menu that you've been accustomed to using.

This is the **TypeTamer control panel.** *It's very self-explanatory: add new categories, choose the typefaces to display in each category, type in the sample text you want to display, choose the type size to display in, and choose how many fonts you want to appear at the top of the font menu.*

Once you install TypeTamer, you can instantly get this control panel right from within your application—you'll see a menu item for it in your font menu, as shown on the opposite page.

104

The TypeTamer menu

TypeTamer changes your font menu, as you can see below. At the top of the list are the fonts used in the document. In the middle of the list are the categories of fonts you created, using the TypeTamer control panel. At the bottom of the list you see the choice "TypeTamer," which you can use to go to the control panel at any time.

TypeTamer scans your document and places the fonts that are actually used in the document at the top of the list, where they are easily accessible. The faces are sorted into families, each with their own submenu.

These are the categories you created in the control panel. A font may be in more than one category.

These are the fonts in the Font Book category, the ones I use in this book. Rather than having to search through a long list, the fonts I need for the book are grouped together. (In this example, these fonts are also shown at the top of the font list anyway because the document for this book is open.)

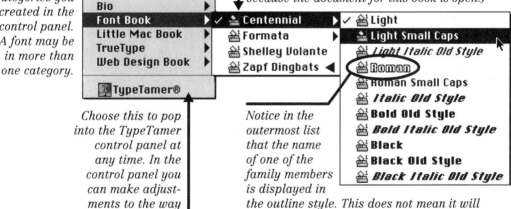

Choose this to pop into the TypeTamer control panel at any time. In the control panel you can make adjustments to the way you want to see things.

Notice in the outermost list that the name of one of the family members is displayed in the outline style. This does not mean it will appear on your page in the outline style! It means that if you don't want to go all the way out to that final menu, you can choose the font name from the middle list, and TypeTamer will automatically select the font that is displayed in the outline style.

In this example, for instance, you could choose Centennial from the middle list, and what would appear on your page is Centennial Roman, not Light or Bold Old Style or Black. It would not appear in the outline style!

Special features of TypeTamer

These two pages show some of the special features of the TypeTamer menu.

*These **icons** tell you whether the font is TrueType, PostScript Type 1 or 3, or bitmapped.*

If a font displays only a bitmap icon, as shown here for Bills Brackets, it means there is no printer font available on the computer. If it's a PostScript font, remember, it won't print properly without its printer font.

(Now, there might be, as in the case here of Avant Garde and Bookman, a printer font resident in the PostScript printer. So even though only the bitmap will display on the screen, the font will print to a PostScript printer beautifully.)

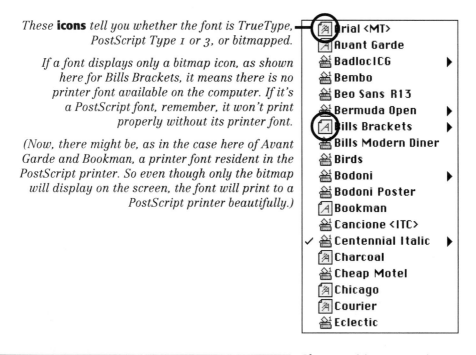

```
⊛ Arial <MT>
⊠ Avant Garde
🗠 BadlocICG                    ▶
🗠 Bembo
🗠 Beo Sans R13
🗠 Bermuda Open                 ▶
🅰 Bills Brackets               ▶
🗠 Bills Modern Diner
🗠 Birds
🗠 Bodoni                       ▶
🗠 Bodoni Poster
🅰 Bookman
🗠 Cancione <ITC>
✓ 🗠 Centennial Italic          ▶
⊛ Charcoal
🗠 Cheap Motel
⊛ Chicago
⊛ Courier
🗠 Eclectic
```

```
Tapioca <ITC>-Regular   Type: PostScript
⊛ IT'S VERY SIMPLE—either you run or you
get busy.
⊛ IT'S VERY SIMPLE—either
you run or you get busy.
```

If you position your pointer over the icon in the font menu, you'll **see an example of the typeface** *(as shown here). Use the TypeTamer control panel (accessible from the bottom of the font menu) to determine what text is displayed, as well as the size of the type.*

These display boxes also show up when you hold down various keys and press on the tiny icons in the TypeTamer menu.

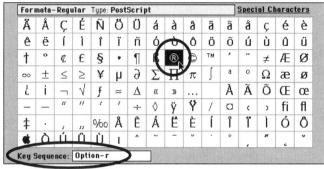

Hold down the **Option** key, position your pointer over the icon in the menu, and you'll get a chart of all the **special characters,** the characters that need the Option or Option-plus-Shift keys to appear. These are the characters such as ©, ™, ®, ¢, and many more.

Slide your pointer over the character you want in your document; let go and that chosen character will appear where the insertion point is flashing in your document. Notice in the bottom-left corner of the display window you see the key combination to type that character.

Besides finding the standard special characters like © and ™, this feature is a great way to find all of those strange characters in picture fonts, ornaments, and dingbats.

In some typefaces, such as picture fonts and ornaments, you want to see not only the special characters, but the **regular characters** as well, the ones you can get by just typing regular letters, capital letters, or numbers. Hold down both the **Option** and the **Command** keys to see the regular characters.

107

WYSIWYG Menus

Favorite features: *Hot keys to change typefaces; customized grouping of fonts; can change color and size of any font in the menu.*

Now WYSIWYG Menus   Now Menus

WYSIWYG Menus (pronounced "wizziwig," and stands for "what you see is what you get") from Now Utilities is one utility in a package of about eight. You can't buy WYSIWYG Menus separately from the rest of the utilities, but you will probably like many of the other things that come with the package anyway.

Create your own groups for your fonts (see the examples); customize the size, color, and typeface of the appearance of each font name in the menu; and even customize the font choices in individual applications.

If you also install the utility called NowMenus (which comes in the package), you can assign hot keys to your fonts! This lets you change typefaces simply by pressing a key combination that you set up yourself.

Hold the pointer over a button to get a little message about what that button does.

To create groups, *double-click on the font name in the right-hand list to bring up the Font Info dialog box (below). Type the group name you want in "Family." Type the actual font name in "Style." Every font under the same Family name will appear as a group. (See the example of "Fun fonts" on the facing page, top left.)*

Select a font, then use the buttons in the toolbar above to customize the size, color, etc.

Since the font Scarlett is all caps, I typed the Font Info/Style name all caps so it will appear properly in the menu.

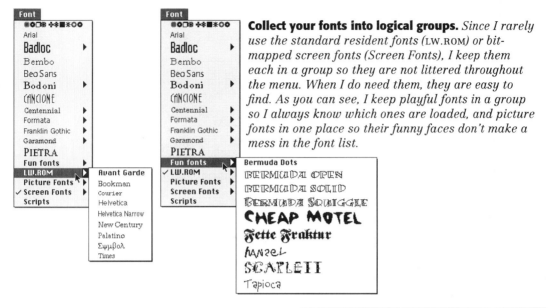

Collect your fonts into logical groups. *Since I rarely use the standard resident fonts (LW.ROM) or bit-mapped screen fonts (Screen Fonts), I keep them each in a group so they are not littered throughout the menu. When I do need them, they are easy to find. As you can see, I keep playful fonts in a group so I always know which ones are loaded, and picture fonts in one place so their funny faces don't make a mess in the font list.*

You can customize the font menu in individual applications, *so even though a number of typefaces may be open, only selected ones will appear in that application's menu.*

One of the options in this "Applications" menu (circled) is "Edit...." Choose "Edit...," then choose an application whose font menu you want to customize. I limit the fonts in Netscape's menu while I am on the Internet.

Any fonts you uncheck are still loaded into the System, they just won't appear in the font menu in the chosen application.

It's so easy **to make a hot key** *that lets you change selected text with a keystroke. Just go to the font menu, highlight the font of your choice, and while it is highlighted (don't let go of the mouse), type the keyboard shortcut you want. You can use any Fkey from F5 through F15, or any key combination that includes a modifier key (Command, Control, Option, or Shift). Just make sure you don't use a key combination that is already used by your application for something else.*

To remove a hot key, *select its font in the font menu, keep the mouse button down, and press the Delete key.*

MenuFonts

MenuFonts

Favorite features: *Inexpensive, small, and easy to use; can customize color, name, and size of fonts to make them easy to find in the menu; can view enlarged characters.*

MenuFonts, from Dubl-Click Software, is sweet and easy to use. It displays the fonts in their own typefaces, groups families together, and shows an icon representing the format of the font (PostScript, TrueType, bitmap, or Multiple Master). You can also color individual font names, change their sizes in the menu, change the name that

displays in the menu, and choose to display the font in another face so you see the name "Zapf Dingbats" instead of "✳︎❂▢✤ ✦✳︎■✳︎✑ ❂❂▼▲" in the menu. MenuFonts is a control panel, so you just drop the control panel on your System Folder, restart, and it works. The control panel and its options are shown on the facing page.

The Bermuda family name in the main menu is displaying in its own face, but I told the other members of the family to display in Geneva so I could read their names on the screen.

I should tell this font, Birds, to display its name in Geveva so I can see the name "Birds" instead of these unintelligible scribbles.

There is an optional strip down the edge of the menu, called the **FontShow Bar.** *Position your pointer over the bar to see information about the font (shown to the right), as well as text in a variety of sizes. You can customize the text that displays.*

Bermuda Dots
PostScript (Type 1)
Font ID: 9890
In file:"Bermuda family screen fonts"
PSprinter file:"BermuDot"

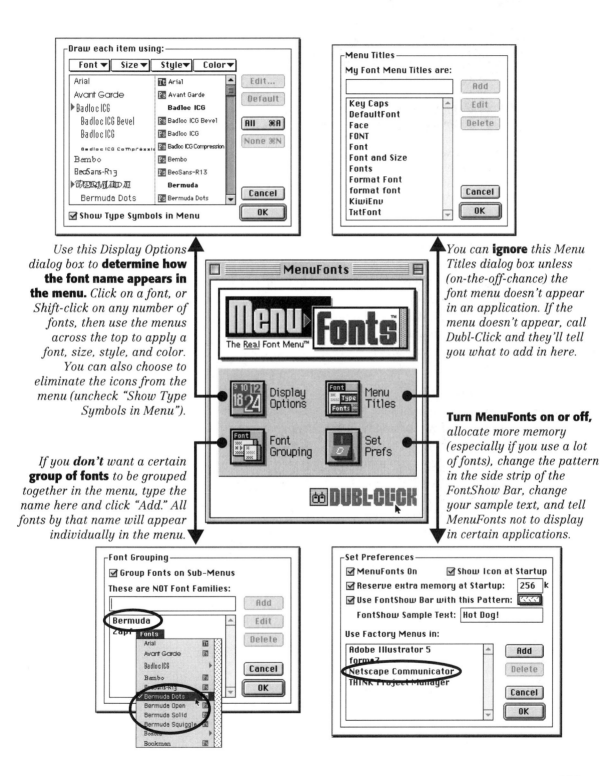

*Use this Display Options dialog box to **determine how the font name appears in the menu.** Click on a font, or Shift-click on any number of fonts, then use the menus across the top to apply a font, size, style, and color. You can also choose to eliminate the icons from the menu (uncheck "Show Type Symbols in Menu").*

*If you **don't** want a certain **group of fonts** to be grouped together in the menu, type the name here and click "Add." All fonts by that name will appear individually in the menu.*

*You can **ignore** this Menu Titles dialog box unless (on-the-off-chance) the font menu doesn't appear in an application. If the menu doesn't appear, call Dubl-Click and they'll tell you what to add in here.*

Turn MenuFonts on or off, *allocate more memory (especially if you use a lot of fonts), change the pattern in the side strip of the FontShow Bar, change your sample text, and tell MenuFonts not to display in certain applications.*

Adobe Type Reunion Deluxe

Favorite features: *Groups of fonts; font can be in more than one group; most recently used font appears at top of menu; can select which font group to appear towards top of menu; can open ATM font sets from menu.*

Adobe Type Reunion Deluxe

Until recently, the simplest and easiest way to fix your font menu was to drop the extension **Adobe Type Reunion** (ATR) onto your System Folder and restart. It gathered all the fonts of one family and put them in one place with a submenu to access the rest of the family members.

Unfortunately, you can't get the almost-free extension anymore. Adobe does sells the Adobe Type Reunion *Deluxe* version (which is great) of this utility, but if you are feeling overwhelmed by all this type stuff and just want a quick and perfectly wonderful fix, see if you can find the simple ATR extension—check with your local Mac User Group, friends, Adobe, etc. You might even have it on your computer or on an Adobe CD somewhere and just don't know it. Use Find File to search for **reunion.** If you find the icon, drop it onto your System Folder and restart. It just works all by itself.

Type Reunion

This is what the ATR extension icon looks like.

Adobe Type Reunion Deluxe is an application that not only organizes your menu, but gives you several options for managing that menu.

As you see in the example below, you can customize the font menu into groups, such as City Names, Display, Script, etc. Or you might want to group them into the projects you're working on. The group called "Active Fonts" is a default list of every font that is loaded at the moment.

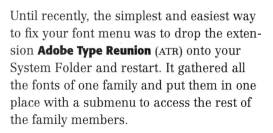

If you choose "Show City Names," the fonts in that group will appear at the top of the list. Notice the bullet (•) before the group "Font Book"? That indicates that I chose to "Show Font Book," and those fonts are listed at the top of the menu.

The ATR Deluxe control panel:

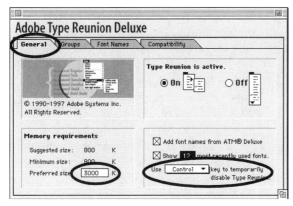

If you use a lot of fonts at one time, open the control panel, choose the General section, and **allocate more memory** *in the "Preferred size" box so ATR can display all of the fonts in their faces.*

Take note of which key to use to **temporarily disable Type Reunion** *(you can change the key). When you use Netscape or Internet Explorer, be sure to use this key to disable Type Reunion before you change your font default in the browser or you'll probably crash.*

As soon as you use a font, its name appears at the extreme top of the list. This is cool. You get really used to it.

In the Font Names section of the control panel, take a look at the two checkboxes at the top. You can choose whether or not to see the fonts in the menu in their actual typeface, and whether or not to view their "preferred" names. The "preferred" name is whatever appears in the right-hand side of the list. **To change that preferred name,** *just click on a font name, even if it's gray, in the right-hand column, and edit or retype. This is a great way to make sure your font names make sense, or to get rid of characters you don't need to see in your menu.*

Notice I unchecked the box next to "Mini Pics" so those font names will show up in Geneva instead of in the dingbat characters they are.

— continued

You can open the Type Reunion control panel from the font menu, and you can **open any of the sets you created in Adobe Type Manager Deluxe** *as well, without having to open the actual ATM Deluxe program.*

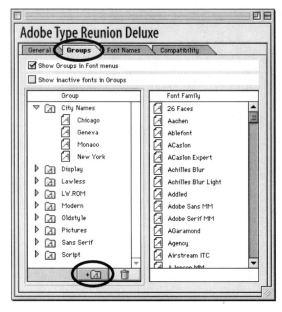

To make new groups *in ATR Deluxe, open the Groups section of the control panel.*

> *Click the folder icon on the bottom left to make a new folder.*
>
> *Rename the folder. Whatever you name this folder will become the group name.*

To add fonts to this group, *drag them from the list on the right-hand side and drop them into the folder on the left.*

> *You can put the same font in more than one group, because the name in the group is not really the actual font, it is just a pointer to the font (sort of like an alias on the Mac Desktop).*

To edit an existing folder/group name, *click once on its name and retype.*

To remove *an entire folder or individual fonts within a folder, select the folder or font, then click on the trash can icon at the bottom of the left-hand list.*

If your ATR control panel has white boxes in it, as shown to the left, it's due to the Mac's "platinum" effect. If it bothers you, go to the Appearance control panel and uncheck "System-wide platinum appearance."

Problems with fonts

Font ID conflicts, merged fonts, and corrupt fonts

Font ID conflicts

What are font ID conflicts?

Each font is identified within the computer by a certain **number** (its **font ID number**), as well as by its **name.** Because there is a limit to the numbers available, and (more relevantly) because there are so many new fonts being created every day and so many vendors, it is possible for two or more fonts to have the same number. This causes an identity crisis. You might choose the font Bembo, but get the font Blackoak on the screen. Or you might open the suitcase Jenson, but it doesn't appear in your menu.

How do you avoid font ID conflicts?

All of the font management utilities, as well as the Macintosh operating system itself, now have automatic features that resolve **numbering conflicts,** so font identification conflicts don't cause the problems they used to. Unless you have very old fonts (like ten years old), you should not experience the ID number problem. If you do have very old fonts and you experience conflicts, I must recommend that you upgrade your fonts.

Avoiding conflicts of name

You can easily avoid the conflicts that happen when you accidentally open two fonts with the same **name** by organizing your fonts the way I recommended in the beginning of this book. These are the basic guidelines to remember:

- Make sure all screen font members of one family are stored in one suitcase; don't put part of the Times family in one suitcase and part in another (the only exception to this is if you have an extraordinarily large family that you never need to have all open at the same time—then go ahead and separate them into two or more suitcases).

- Make sure you have only one copy of the family on your hard disk—don't keep a copy in your good fonts folder, plus a copy in your System Folder.

- Don't put copies of the same font into more than one suitcase.

- Don't use two fonts at the same time with the same name, even if they are from two different vendors.

- *Never rename a printer font!*

Merged fonts

Merged fonts in the menu

You may have noticed that some font families have one listing in the font menu, such as Times, yet you can create *true-drawn* versions (as opposed to fake versions) of italic, bold, and bold italic by choosing those styles from a menu or by applying keyboard shortcuts.

Other font families have a separate font in the menu for each separate style: there is Garamond, Garamond Italic, Garamond Bold, and Garamond Bold Italic. If you try to select a word in Garamond and apply the keyboard shortcut to make it italic, it may appear slanted on the screen but it does not print italic; it is a "false" style.

And separate fonts might appear in odd places on your menu. Some of the bold fonts (but not all) start with B Garamond Bold, B Bodoni Bold, etc. So some of the bold fonts get grouped together, some of the italic fonts get grouped together, some fonts are grouped together by name, and you have to track down the oddballs that show up in odd places. For instance, Extrabold Goudy is at the bottom of the list under "XB Goudy." And having all these stupid names in the list makes the list interminably long, as shown to the right.

Now, Chapter 13 is all about font menu utilities that make your menu more *manageable*. But even if it's manageable, you need to understand about **merged fonts.** If a vendor has merged a font, you won't see a separate menu item for Times Italic, Times Bold, or Times Bold Italic. You will only see "Times," and you just have to *know* that you can use keyboard shortcuts to apply the italic and bold.

So in the next column are examples of the kinds of things that drive us nuts about fonts.

Centennial Light
Centennial Italic using keyboard
Centennial Italic true-drawn
Centennial Bold using keyboard
Centennial Bold true-drawn
I can use the keyboard shortcut to make Centennial Italic (notice the italic characters are different from the regular characters, they're not just slanted). But I can't use the shortcut to make the Bold. See how the Bold is so clunky and dorky? That's the clue that it is not "true-drawn." I must choose Centennial Bold from the font menu to get the true Bold version.

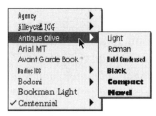

Here Adobe Type Reunion has grouped the family Antique Olive together. But I only see six members of the family. I remember that when I organized my fonts, I found eight members of Antique Olive. Where are they?

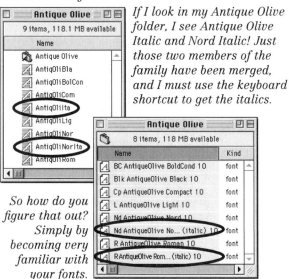

If I look in my Antique Olive folder, I see Antique Olive Italic and Nord Italic! Just those two members of the family have been merged, and I must use the keyboard shortcut to get the italics.

So how do you figure that out? Simply by becoming very familiar with your fonts.

Advantages and disadvantages of merged fonts

It is nice of font vendors to merge fonts for you because it makes it easier to work. But the disadvantage is that you have no clue as to the actual styles available. This is another good reason for you to simply get to know your fonts better. As you organize them (as explained in Chapter 11), you will see exactly how many members are in each font. When you find a font in your menu like Antique Olive that has no italic version showing, you will probably remember seeing italic versions when you sorted the font family, so you will know you can use the shortcut.

Hierarchical menu is not merged

Just because you see *hierarchical menus* (the ones that pop out from little triangles) in your font list does not mean the fonts are *merged.* There are several utilities that create these hierarchical menus, as explained in Chapter 13.

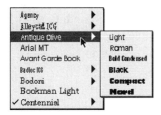

In this example you see the family Antique Olive grouped together in a hierarchical menu by a font menu utility (Adobe Type Reunion, in this case). This is not "merged"! But the two individual faces Roman and Nord are merged with their individual italic versions, which means you can use the keyboard shortcut to make those faces italic and you will get a true-drawn italic, not just a fake, slanted face.

So what to do?

You have to be conscious of merged and not merged faces in your fonts menu so you can choose the correct one for your job.

To print to your own printer: If you use a keyboard shortcut to make a font bold, italic, etc., and you print to your own printer and it prints just fine, then go ahead and use the keyboard shortcuts.

To print at a service bureau: If you ever plan to take the project to a service bureau for high-resolution output, always choose the styled font from the menu (unless you can't because the vendor merged it), not the keyboard shortcut.

To go cross-platform: If your files have to go to a PC (a Windows machine), *you should use the keyboard shortcut!* It might make the type look stupid on your Macintosh screen and it might not print properly from your Mac, but the typeface styles are not named exactly the same across the two platforms. That is, if you're using Garamond and choose I Garamond Italic, it is most likely that when that font gets to the Windows machine, the italic version is not named I Garamond Italic, so the wrong font appears. Use the keyboard shortcut.

What I do: I typically use the keyboard shortcut to change the style as I'm working, then when I'm done with the project I search and replace: I search for anything with the shortcut italic, replace that with the true italic version of the typeface, and remove the shortcut italic style. Most programs can do this easily in search-and-replace (often called find-and-change).

Corrupt fonts

How to tell if a font is corrupt

It's not uncommon for fonts to become corrupt for no reason that you can tell. They just do that sometimes. A corrupt font can cause terrible problems in your computer, from crashing files to crashing your entire system. The three most common ways to tell if a font is corrupt are 1) if you choose a typeface from your font menu and your entire document crashes, 2) the typeface looks fine on the screen but the job refuses to print (while other files without that font print fine), or 3) you look in the folder at the file and it no longer has an icon, it's just blank (as shown below).

If a font doesn't print correctly or if it looks bad on the screen, that does not necessarily mean it's corrupt—it might just mean you are missing the printer font.

Font Reserve, MasterJuggler, and ATM Deluxe check for corruption or damage in a font and won't load a bad one. Suitcase, however, will let you load corrupt fonts. The System Folder will let you add corrupt fonts to the Fonts folder, but often won't let you take them back out.

What to do about it

If you suspect a bad font may be giving you trouble, look in its folder. Most of the time a corrupt font will have a blank look, its icon missing. In fact, while you are in the process of organizing your fonts, you should remove any printer font, bitmap, or TrueType font with a blank icon. If it's a PostScript font, remove both parts of the matching pair, even if only one of the pieces is bad. Reinstall from the original disks.

Sometimes a font is so corrupt that it is literally impossible to remove it from the Fonts folder in the System Folder. You might get a message telling you the file is damaged and cannot be moved. Try renaming it, then tossing it. If that doesn't work, try to move the bad font to the Desktop, restart, and then try to throw it in the trash and empty the trash. If you can't do that, try moving it from the Fonts folder into the System Folder and restarting, then see if you can remove the bad font. If even that fails, you will have to restart from another disk, like your System tools CD, remove and trash the corrupt font, then restart with your internal System.

Uxorious 24

Uxorious 24

A good, healthy font has some sort of icon. Either it has one A, three As, or it is some sort of printer font icon (as shown on page 25).

*Also notice on bitmaps and TrueType icons that the **upper LEFT corner** is turned down. Only fonts have the upper left corner turned down.*

If a font is completely blank, this is one clue that it's bad. Throw it away immediately and empty the trash. If the blank file has a matching PostScript file, throw that one away also and reinstall from the original disks.

*Also notice that the **upper RIGHT corner** of this file is turned down, another clue that this is not a healthy font.*

Printing fonts at a service bureau

What is a service bureau?

A service bureau is a shop where they have computers (mostly Macs) and printers, just like you, but their main printer is about $100,000 more expensive than yours. They print to this printer (or to their color printers or laser printers) just like you print to your printer: they put your disk in their Macintosh, copy the document and the fonts you provide onto their hard drive, load the fonts and open the document, and print. This large printer, which is usually called an *imagesetter,* prints pages onto resin-coated paper rather than onto plain paper. Imagesetters are always PostScript-based. If you have never taken your work to an imagesetter and if you don't plan to for a while, go back to your coffee. You don't need to read this right now.

But if you have ever taken work to a service bureau, you know that a problem comes up around fonts. Service bureaus have a certain number and variety of fonts to use on their machine. They might even have fonts with the same names as the fonts in your publications. But, if they have fonts from one vendor and you have fonts from another vendor, even though they have the same name, you can have major problems.

See, you might have used the font Futura in your document. You call your service bureau before you take it there and they say, oh yes, we have Futura. But your Futura is from Bitstream and their Futura is from Adobe. Even though they have the same name, they have subtle design differences and, more importantly, they have different *font metrics* which affect the word spacing, the letter spacing, the line spacing, and other features. Not only can the wrong font give you bad spacing and the wrong line breaks, it can give you totally unacceptable type, ruining your entire job.

Another common problem is that your service bureau might not have equivalent fonts at all. For instance, my service bureau does not own the Linotype Centennial family complete with the small caps and oldstyle collections. Nor do they have Formata or Eclectic or Scarlett or Shelley. And you know (because you read the previous part of this book) that the Mac must have both the screen font and the printer font to display and print the job. So whaddya do?

One thing to do is call your service bureau before you take the job in and discuss the project before problems arise.

Take your fonts to the service bureau

For years you weren't supposed to take your fonts to your service bureau so they can print with them—it was technically considered illegal. The legality of this has been changing, though, because there is no other way to ensure that your job prints properly. There are still some gray areas, but the black-and-white reality is that you must take your fonts to the service bureau. That's the way it is. Every service bureau cannot own every font under the sun. The service bureau loads your fonts up and prints your job; when the job is finished, they remove the fonts from their computer. If they don't remove the fonts from their computer, then they are stealing those fonts and you should not take your work there anymore. (Some fonts are *freeware* or *shareware* and can be passed around; if it is shareware, please respect the small fee.)

How do you take your fonts to the service bureau?

You followed the directions in the first part of this book for organizing your fonts into their separate folders, right? If you really did, then this is easy: simply copy the folders that contain the screen and printer fonts onto an extra floppy disk or onto the hard disk cartridge you are taking to the service bureau. Every service bureau uses a font management utility and they can just open the suitcases with the click of a button. Font Reserve and MasterJuggler have special features that make it even easier for you to gather the fonts that belong to a job.

To make it easier for the service bureau, make one folder on the disk you're taking; for now let's call it "Fonts to Go." Then copy, *not* the entire font family folder itself, but just the **contents** of your font family folder into the "Fonts to Go" folder on the disk. This means "Fonts to Go" will contain a variety of loose suitcases and printer fonts, which means your service bureau can open all of the suitcases quicker and easier.

If you really wanna be nice and don't have an excessive number of fonts in your document, you can make one new suitcase for them. Copy all the fonts **you actually used** into this one suitcase. In many families of fonts, you don't use every member of the family. For instance, you might have used just the ultra bold, but not the italics or light weights. So copy just the ultra bold screen font into the new suitcase, and copy just the ultra bold printer font into the same folder where you have this suitcase. Then your service bureau only has to open one suitcase. Oh, you are so nice! *But don't leave that conglomerate suitcase on your hard disk, because then you have the same font in more than one place and you could develop problems!*

On the disk you take to your service bureau, label the disk and files very clearly! Don't leave superfluous junk on the disk that has nothing to do with your project.

A few extra font utilities for you

There are a number of great little font utilities that can make life with fonts easier. All of the items in this chapter are available on the Internet and can be downloaded—look for them at www.shareware.com. The individual vendor information is also available on page 142. The utilities are almost all shareware, so be sure to read the ReadMe files and to send in the small shareware fees. Some products are limited in their features until you send in your fees. Have fun!

Apple's **Key Caps** is a font utility that is most likely sitting on your Mac right now. Once you open it, you get a new menu item called Key Caps, which is a list of your installed fonts. Choose a font to see its characters in this display. Hold down the Shift key to see Shift characters (such as a capital G or an *); hold down the Option key to see Option characters (such as •, ¢, ™, or ©); hold down Shift and Option together to see Shift-Option characters (such as ¿ or ±).

Key Caps does not type these in your document for you—you just have to find the character you want (if you can see things that small), find the key combination that types that character, then go back to your document, choose that font, and type the combination (or you can copy and paste, as long as you use the same font in your document). Whew. There are easier ways to find and type special characters—read on.

PopChar Lite

PopChar Lite

Favorite features: *Free; easy to use; easy access to all characters, even those that require multiple keystrokes.*

PopChar Lite is the free version of this great utility. It shows you every character built into a selected font, including all those special characters that are hard to find, and it shows you which keys to press to type that character. Or if you don't want to type it yourself, just slide the pointer over the character you want, let go, and that character will appear in your document (it appears on your page wherever the insertion point is flashing).

PopChar is a control panel—drop it on your System Folder, restart, and it works. In your application, choose the font, then open PopChar.

PopChar is pronounced "pop care," because the "char" is short for "character."

*Below is the **PopChar Lite control panel.** The "hot spot" is where you press to display the PopChar chart; set it to your favorite position. I set my "preferred font sizes" starting with the largest so if the font is installed in that size, PopChar will display the characters in that size.*

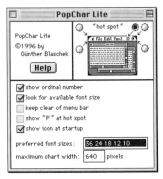

To use PopChar, *open the application you want to work in. PopChar will display (as shown above) whatever font is selected, or the font that is directly to the left of the flashing insertion point, or any font you choose from the font menu (but don't move the insertion point after you choose a new font).* **Press on the hot spot** *you've set up in the control panel, and you'll get the PopChar display. Slide your pointer over the character you want, let go, and there it is in your document. Too cool. Notice that the top-right corner tells you which keys to type to set that character.*

122

PopChar Pro

Favorite features: *Customizable layouts for individual fonts; can view any size font, even if that size is not installed; detachable and resizable.*

PopChar Pro

PopChar Pro is the expanded version of PopChar Lite. It comes with a 20–page user's guide, so I'll just tell you the highlights here. The display window can "float" so you can leave it open and accessible all the time. You can choose from a variety of layout options (the example below is showing "Letters in Groups"), and you can customize the layout and the font size for each installed font! Be sure to read the user's guide for details.

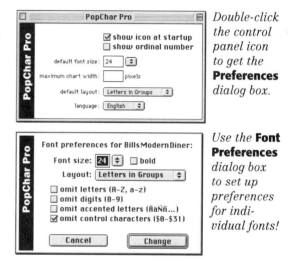

Double-click the control panel icon to get the **Preferences** *dialog box.*

Use the **Font Preferences** *dialog box to set up preferences for individual fonts!*

```
Fri 1:10p.m.  [P] 📞 [P]
```

This is how the **PopChar icon** *appears in your menu. Press on it to make the window appear.*

Before you detach the window, press here to get the **Font Preferences** *dialog box (shown above, right) for the displayed font.*

*If your pointer is **not** positioned over a character, you will see* **"Open Window"** *in this area, instead of a character. Click on it to detach the window and let it float.*

Once the window is detached, you can click the zoom box in the bottom-left corner to **resize** *it to the tiny box shown above.*

KeyCap

Favorite features: *Prints hard copy of all keystrokes to type all characters; can see characters you didn't know were in the font.*

KeyCap

The small program called **KeyCap** from Adobe is not the same as the Apple desk accessory named "Key Caps" that you have in your Apple menu—this KeyCap program is much more useful. If you have Adobe products, you might have this on your hard disk already. Open it and choose any installed font to get the chart you see opposite. This chart tells you how to type any character in the typeface. Print the chart—the printout looks just like the one you see here. This is very handy. (FontBook, page 128, can also print a similar chart.)

Click on any character to see it displayed in a separate box, as shown here. You can, obviously, click the buttons to enlarge or reduce the character.

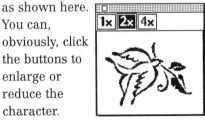

KeyCap Map System 8.0 - English

Key	None	Shift	Option	Opt-Shft	Key	None	Shift	Option	Opt-Shft
a		A	∫	Å	`	`	~		`
b		B	(		1	1	!		/
c		C	(	Ç	2	2	@		¤
d		D	∂	Î	3	3	#	£	‹
e	f	E		‰	4	4	$	¢	›
f		F	ƒ	Ï	5	5	%	∞	fI
g		G	©		6	6	^	§	fL
h		H		Ó	7	7	&	¶	‡
i		I		â	8	8	*	•	°
j		J	Δ	ô	9	9	(	ª	·
k	K	K	¬		0	0	)	º	,
l		L	¬	Ò	-	-	_	–	—
m	M	M	µ	Â	=	=	+	≠	±
n		N			[	[	{	"	"
o		O		Ø	]	]	}	'	'
p		P	π	∏	'	'	"		fE
q	Q	Q		Œ	;	;	:	…	Ú
r	R	R	«	‰	\	\		«	»
s		S	ß	Í	,	,	<	≤	¸
t		T	†		.	.	>	≥	·
u		U			/	/	?	÷	¿
v		V	√	◊					
w	W	W	Σ	„					
x		X	≈	"					
y		Y	¥	Á					
z		Z	Ω						

1st Key	+ 2nd Key Composite Character						
	e	u	i	o	a	Spc	y,n
Option + `							
Option + e							
Option + u							
Option + i							

Font Name: **Cancione ITC** Font Type: **Type 1** ID#: **12137**

FontView

Favorite features: *Can display a font even if it's not loaded; can enlarge individual characters or entire set; provides lots of info about fonts.*

FontView

FontView is a shareware utility that displays the characters in a selected font. Double-click on any character to see it larger and to get information about it.

Below you see the FontView window. A wonderful thing about this program is that you can view the characters of fonts that are not even loaded in your System! This is great for looking at new typefaces on CDs, taking a look at fonts whose faces you can't remember, etc. Use the FontView menu to get all sorts of information about the type.

*Use the "FontView" menu to get all kinds of **information** about the selected font.*

*Use the File menu to **open** the suitcase of **a font that is not in your font menu** (which means it's not loaded into the System).*

*Double-click a character to see it **enlarged.** Type any character and it will then appear in this box.*

Click *a letter and it will appear in the edit box at the bottom, or* **type** *in the edit box and the characters in the display will be selected.*

TypeIndexer

Favorite features: *Prints hard copy of font in various layouts; can print fonts even if they are not loaded; can print more than one font sample per page.*

TypeIndexer

TypeIndexer will print a collection of all of your fonts. It can also run an error check to see if any of your fonts are defective.

- Use the "Select…" button in the TypeIndexer dialog box to choose the fonts you want to print.

- Use the "Page Template" menu to choose the layout of the printed pages. The example on the next page uses the "4 per page" layout.

- Read the ReadMe file to learn the various ways to check for font corruption.

- Check "About TypeIndexer…" from the Apple menu for quick-start directions.

```
1 per page
2 per page
4 per page
6 per page
15 per page
Character Chart
1 Cap Height Calculator
✓ 1 Graduated
1 Point Rule
1 Style Samples
1 Up Display
15 Up Plain
15 Up/path
20 per page
40 per page
60 per page
```

These are the **page layout options.** *Experiment with each of them before you decide to print out an entire batch of fonts.*

These are the **Preferences.** *Click "Use error checking" as one method to find corrupt fonts.*

TypeIndexer Preferences

Header:

Footer:

Custom Text for samples…

Whatever you type in this box will appear in your printed demo pages! Hey Mom, what's up?

☐ Record font downloads ☐ Print to disk
☑ Use error checking

Cancel   OK

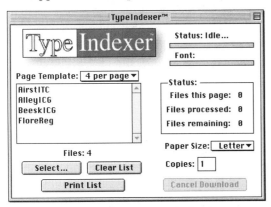

This is the **TypeIndexer** *main dialog box.*

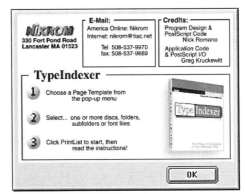

This is the "About" box with **quick-start** *directions.*

AirstreamITC

ABCDEFGHIJKLMNOPQRSTU
VWXYZabcdefghijklmnopqrstuvw
xyz1234567890-=!@#$%^&*()_

Whatever you type in this box will appear in your
printed demo pages! Hey Mom, what's up? Whatever
you type in this box will appear in your printed demo
pages! Hey Mom, what's up? Whatever you type in this
box will appear in your printed demo pages! Hey Mom,
what's up? Whatever you type in this box will appear in
your printed demo pages! Hey Mom, what's up? Whatever you type in this box will appear in your printed

AirstITC   10/12

AlleycatICG

ABCDEFGHIJKLMNOPQRSTUVWXYZab
cdefghijklmnopqrstuvwxyz1234567
890=!@#$% ^&*()_+

Whatever you type in this box will appear in your
printed demo pages! Hey Mom, what's up? Whatever
you type in this box will appear in your printed demo
pages! Hey Mom, what's up? Whatever you type in this
box will appear in your printed demo pages! Hey Mom,
what's up? Whatever you type in this box will appear
in your printed demo pages! Hey Mom, what's up?
Whatever you type in this box will appear in your

AlleyICG   10/12

BeeskneesICG

ABCDEFGHIJKLMNOPQRSTU
VWXYZABCDEFGHIJKLMN
OPQRSTUVWXYZ 12345678
90=!@#!%^?*()_+

WHATEVER YOU TYPE IN THIS BOX WILL
APPEAR IN YOUR PRINTED DEMO PAGES!
HEY MOM, WHAT'S UP? WHATEVER YOU
TYPE IN THIS BOX WILL APPEAR IN YOUR
PRINTED DEMO PAGES! HEY MOM, WHAT'S
UP? WHATEVER YOU TYPE IN THIS BOX
WILL APPEAR IN YOUR PRINTED DEMO
PAGES! HEY MOM, WHAT'S UP? WHATEVE

BeeskICG   10/12

FlorensRegular

ABCDEFGHIJKLMNOPQRSTUVW
XYZabcdefghijklmnopqrstu
vwxyz1234567890=!@#$%^&*()_+

Whatever you type in this box will appear in your printed demo
pages! Hey Mom, what's up? Whatever you type in this box will
appear in your printed demo pages! Hey Mom, what's up?
Whatever you type in this box will appear in your printed demo
pages! Hey Mom, what's up? Whatever you type in this box will
appear in your printed demo pages! Hey Mom, what's up?
Whatever you type in this box will appear in your printed demo
pages! Hey Mom, what's up? Whatever you type in this box will

FloreReg   10/12

This is an example of one of the many formats in which TypeIndexer
can print samples of your fonts. This layout is the "4 per page" option.

FontBook

Favorite features: *Prints hard copy of font in various layouts, including a key code for special characters; can print fonts even if they are not loaded; can see preview of page before it prints.*

FontBook

FontBook will help you make a catalog of your entire type library with a variety of flexible layouts that display the font in various ways, such as by size, in long paragraphs of text, a reference card of key combinations to type special characters, and more. On the opposite page are examples of some of the layouts.

As usual, read the ReadMe file that came with the software for more details. In the case of FontBook, the ReadMe file is called "Documentation."

Font
Other Font...	⌘F
Previous Font	⌘–
Next Font	⌘+
Arial	
Avant Garde	

Use the "Font" menu to **choose the font** *to display and print. Also from this menu, choose "Other Font..." to select a typeface that is not currently loaded.*

File
Save as...	⌘S
Close	⌘W
Page Setup...	
Print One	
Print...	⌘P
MultiPrint...	⌘M
Quit	⌘Q

Use the "File" menu to choose to **print more than one** *typeface at a time, whether it is loaded or not. To select more than one font from the list if the font names are not next to each other, hold down the Command key while you click on each name.*

Layout
✓ Reference	⌘1
Fontsizes	⌘2
Fontstyles	⌘3
ASCII Table	⌘4
Overview	⌘5
More Fontsizes	⌘6
More Fontsizes (II.)	⌘7
Long Text	⌘8
6 x 6	
Black Boxes	
Black Circles	
UpperCase/LowerCase	

Use the "Layout" menu to choose a **layout.** *You will see an instant* **preview,** *as shown on the opposite page. Click in the bottom-left corner of the preview to change the magnification of the* **preview** *(not of the printed page).*

Edit
Undo	⌘Z
Cut	⌘X
Copy	⌘C
Paste	⌘U
Clear	
Preferences ▶	

Use the "Edit" menu to **customize the Preferences.** *It's especially fun to change the sample text that prints.*

Sample Text...	
Footer Line...	
Magnification...	⌘#
✓ Frames	⌘R
Gray Boxes	⌘G
✓ Pathname	⌘N
Header Font...	⌘H
Header like Text	⌘T
✓ Justify Left	
Justify Center	
Justify Right	

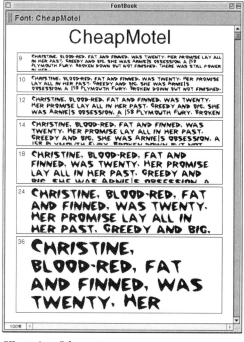

"Fontsizes" layout.

"Overview" layout.

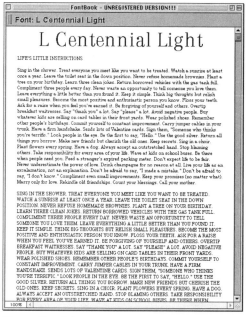

"Long Text" layout.

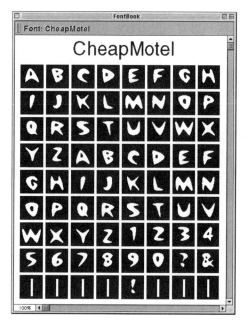

"Black Boxes" layout.

FontLoupe

Favorite features: *Tells which fonts are embedded in the* EPS *graphics that you place in your other applications.*

FontLoupe

FontLoupe is a great little tool that tells you which fonts are embedded within EPS graphics. You see, when you create an EPS graphic within a program like Macromedia FreeHand or Adobe Illustrator, you can, of course, use any font you own. If you send that EPS graphic off to a service bureau to print, or if you put the graphic into a page layout document that you made in Adobe PageMaker or QuarkXPress, the graphic still wants that font you used to create it with (the printer needs the outline, remember?). It's very common to take the graphic to another computer and discover that the graphic looks terrible because the font is missing.

So FontLoupe tells you what font is in the graphic. This way you can make sure you bring it with you to the service bureau, or, if you *are* the service bureau, you know which fonts need to be loaded before you open the job.

To use FontLoupe, just drag any EPS file on top of the FontLoupe icon. You will get a box of info like the one shown above.

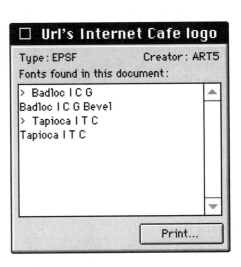

Part IV

Useful Information

This part contains answers to some of the most common problems you may come up against *(help!)*. There is also a chapter on the incredibly cool things you can do with Fontographer, an address list of some of the many font vendors, and various ways to acquire fonts, including freeware and shareware.

Help!!!

If any of these terms or concepts are unfamiliar to you, look them up in the index.

HELP: When I type, the typeface shows up as a bunch of straight lines or boxes!

HELP: When I double-click the screen font to display the typeface, all I see is lines or boxes. Is the font damaged?

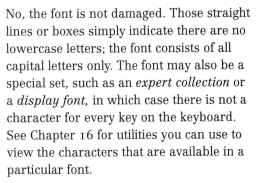

No, the font is not damaged. Those straight lines or boxes simply indicate there are no lowercase letters; the font consists of all capital letters only. The font may also be a special set, such as an *expert collection* or a *display font,* in which case there is not a character for every key on the keyboard. See Chapter 16 for utilities you can use to view the characters that are available in a particular font.

HELP: ATM doesn't seem to be working! My fonts are all jaggy on the screen.

Did you just install ATM? Make sure you: have no older versions of ATM also installed; have not changed the names of any of the ATM files; installed the proper and latest version for your computer and it's installed in the proper place (see next paragraph); ATM is turned on (use the ATM Control Panel); and you have restarted your Mac since you installed ATM.

In OS 8 and later versions of System 7.x, the ATM control panel should be in the Control Panels folder in the System Folder. In System 7.0, the ATM program icon should be in the Control Panels folder, and the *driver* should be loose in the System Folder. If your ATM is named ~ATM, don't remove the tilde (~). That character forces ATM to load into the System last, which it needs to do to work correctly.

You should have current versions of your System software, ATM, and your applications. You can't use new ATM with outdated software and expect it to work flawlessly.

If you've been using ATM for a while and this is a new problem, make sure the fonts in question are open (loaded) and that their *printer fonts* are stored in the proper place, depending on how you have organized your fonts. Check the folder where you store your printer fonts—is there a matching outline printer font for each bitmapped font?

If you just installed new fonts, try restarting the Mac. If you're using MasterJuggler, quit the application and open it back up again.

HELP: In Photoshop, sometimes the bottom or top of a letter is missing.

Quit Photoshop, then open the ATM control panel. Change the option "Preserve" from "Line spacing" to "Character shapes." Restart.

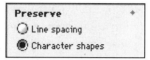

In ATM Deluxe, you'll find this option in the Preferences dialog box, under the File menu.

HELP: ATM works on some fonts, but not others.

If ATM works on some fonts but not others, it probably can't find the printer font for the jaggy ones. Make sure the printer font is stored in the proper place, depending on how you have organized your fonts. Make sure you have a separate printer font for each bitmapped style.

Remember, most *resident fonts* (Avant Garde, Bookman, Palatino, New Century Schoolbook, Zapf Dingbats, Zapf Chancery) don't have *printer fonts* available for ATM unless you have bought and installed them.

HELP: I want to remove the TrueType screen fonts and replace them with the screen fonts for my PostScript fonts (or vice versa), but I can't tell which bitmaps are which.

You're right. You can't. I can't either. The best thing to do is eliminate any font files you're uncertain of, and reinstall the original bitmaps from the original disk (or source) of the PostScript font.

HELP: I think a font must be damaged. What do I do?

After you have determined that it's not a problem with improper installation or anything else, then just throw out the *screen* and *printer fonts* that are on your hard disk and replace them with the originals from your original disk.

HELP: My PostScript fonts show up just fine on the screen but they don't print.

If they appear on the screen just fine, it means they're installed properly. But some older applications or printer drivers look for the printer fonts in the wrong place. If you have an old System or Mac and currently store your printer fonts in the Extensions folder or in the Fonts folder, try moving them into the System Folder, just hanging around loose. This is especially important if you're having trouble printing from old software, or to a printer that uses a special driver.

HELP: My font turns into Courier, Geneva, or Chicago.

When a font turns into Courier, Geneva, or Chicago on the screen, it indicates the bitmapped screen font is missing or damaged. If you use a font management utility (such as ATM Deluxe, Font Reserve, Suitcase, or MasterJuggler), "missing" may mean that it just isn't open—you haven't loaded it yet. If you don't use a font management program and this suddenly happened to your font, or if it really is loaded and still turns into Courier, replace both the bitmap and the printer font with the original from your disk.

HELP: The spacing between words or letters on my printed page looks wrong.

If you try to print city-named fonts to PostScript printers, you will usually get terrible letter and word spacing; change the font to one without a city name.

If you are using a word processor that can use fractional-width spacing, such as Microsoft Word or ClarisWorks, be sure to choose that option before you print to a PostScript printer. In Word, find that option in the Page Setup dialog box; in ClarisWorks, it's in the Preferences dialog box.

A damaged bitmapped font can cause terrible spacing. If you suspect that to be the case, remove all those bitmaps and replace them with the originals from your original disk.

HELP: My justified paragraphs aren't aligned on the right side.

If you are using a word processor that can use fractional-width spacing, such as Microsoft Word or ClarisWorks, be sure to choose the fractional-width spacing option. In Word, find that option in the Page Setup dialog box; in ClarisWorks, it's in the Preferences dialog box. Your text will look even better if you use PostScript fonts and ATM Deluxe after you turn on fractional-width spacing.

If your application does not use fractional-width spacing (which is then called "integer-width" spacing), then install more bitmap sizes of the font.

HELP: The names of my fonts don't appear in the menu.

Check to make sure your fonts are installed properly. If you use a font management utility, make sure the fonts are open. If you use

Word, your font menu (as all other menus) are customizable and the fonts might not be added to the menu yet. Check the Character dialog box (Command D).

Some current software packages and all old software cannot recognize new fonts when you open them through a font management utility while the application is open. Try quitting your application and relaunching.

HELP: I choose my font and then select "Bold" from the menu. It looks bold on the screen, but doesn't print bold.

Most downloadable fonts cannot be changed into bold or italic from the keyboard or the menu; you must instead choose the actual italic or bold font from the menu. You can usually tell on the screen if the computer is faking it. Take a look at the examples below.

This is the regular font.
This is not really bold.
This is the true bold font.

HELP: I downloaded several fonts into my printer, but now they're missing from the printer.

When you manually download fonts, they go into the printer's random access memory, or RAM. Anything in RAM disappears as soon as the machine loses power. So if you have turned off the printer or if there was a power interruption or failure, all those downloaded fonts are gone and you have to download them all over again.

Useful tricks with Fontographer

The program **Fontographer,** from Macromedia Corporation, is the coolest, most incredible program around for people who are interested in or need to work with or play with type. Fontographer is so versatile, so deep, and yet so easy.

I say Fontographer is a very "deep" program because it has all the tools necessary for you to get incredibly complex and to create typefaces of the most exacting and professional standards, but it is also very intuitive and elegant. You can pop into it for five minutes or a couple of hours to create an amazing number of useful and useless characters and fonts, or to tweak existing type to your particular specifications and needs.

I think Fontographer is so useful and so much fun that I added this chapter to give you some ideas for using this great product. I was going to provide step-by-step directions, but their manual does this already, and it's a great manual.

Copyright

Remember, fonts are copyrighted. It's not right to build on someone else's work and then sell it as your own. You might need to tweak a font for your own in-house use, but that doesn't make it yours to sell.

Common solutions

As with any of the font manipulation programs, you can create typefaces in different formats (TrueType, Type 1, Type 3) and for different platforms (Windows, NeXT, Sun, etc.). You can change an existing font from one format into another, such as TrueType into Type 1, or you can change it into the necessary format for another platform.

And you can create all those fractions you need, and add missing bullets, em dashes, slashes, quotation marks, etc., to the freeware fonts you acquired.

More creative solutions

A woman from a company that publishes material for young children needed to change a few characters in the primary serif font they use. The company wanted a one-story "a" (like this: ɑ) and a one-story "g" (like this: ɡ) in their children's learn-to-read books so children would not get confused between the g's and a's they are taught to write and the ones they are taught to read (serif fonts rarely use one-story a's or g's). She used Fontographer to change the forms of those characters to suit the needs of their book publications.

Your signature

If you're good with a mouse or if you have a tablet with a stylus, you can turn your signature into a character. Or if you have a scanner, simply write your name, scan it in, and turn the image into a character. Add it to the font you use for correspondence. Once you've made it, you can copy the signature character and paste it into any font you use regularly so it's always readily available. This is great for adding your signature to faxes that come right out of your computer.

Your handwriting

If you're feeling more ambitious, you can write out the alphabet, scan it in, and make your own handwriting into a font. Then when you write to your grandmother, she won't think it disrespectful that you typed your letter.

Dear Grandma

Rough handlettering

For a more interesting look, draw the alphabet on a paper towel or sandpaper instead of on smooth paper.

Calligraphy

Or you can choose the calligraphic pen tool, choose a stroke width and angle, and draw a calligraphic font directly onto the screen. It's easiest with a tablet and stylus, but you can do interesting things with the mouse.

These fonts are from Foster & Horton

New and useful characters

Jan White once wrote me with this question: "You are too young to remember the 'interrobang' [shown below] which had its fifteen minutes about a generation ago. How can it be resuscitated? Can you make one up and attach it as a pi character? That would be a True Contribution to The Cause! Freeman Craw came up with it, if I remember right."

The answer: Piece o' cake, Jan! (But I thought it was Martin Speckter who came up with it.) Open any font in Fontographer, then just copy the exclamation point and paste it into an available character space. Copy the question mark and copy it into the same space. Eliminate one of the dots, of course, and there you one version of an interrobang.

?! *This is an interrobang, which can be so useful! Of course you would have to make a separate one for each font in which you want to include it.*

Wild and fun fonts

Using Fontographer for specialty, fun fonts is so incredibly easy that you could make it a family project to design a typeface. Creating a specialized typeface could be a project for the high school yearbook class, or your teenager could take some of that teenage energy and design a graffiti font. Below is the typeface my daughter, Scarlett, designed when she was seven years old; it was for the chapter heads in the computer dictionary I wrote (called *Jargon*). She drew each character on tissue paper, then we simply recreated their free forms right on the screen. It's called (of course) "Scarlett" and is available online (www.ratz.com/scarlett/).

THIS IS MY GREAT FONT!

Specialty characters

I had a call from a man who was struggling with typesetting the Hawaiian language with all its accent marks over letters. I suggested he just copy the macrons, copy the characters they belong with, and paste the two of them together into unused character spaces.

pōhaku kī ʻi

A similar use is for people who need to set pronunciations, either in dictionaries or glossaries, or simply within text for difficult words. Make the characters you need by flipping existing characters, copying diacritical marks and pasting them over copies of letters, adding accent marks, making various weights of stress marks, etc.

ser′ən dip′i tē

Customize picture font characters

You can transform picture font characters to suit your fancy. For instance, I love the font Printers Ornaments M from Richard Beatty Designs. But all these wonderful characters are men. I copied one, pasted it into an unused space, adjusted a few points, and now I have this nice female figure also.

Create special characters for logos

You can create your own swashes or specially adapted characters to act as part of your logotype.

I copied this letter "o," then copied the bird (from the font Birds) on top of it. Now I can use this extra fancy "o" wherever I want.

Make your own blats

It takes about one minute to make your own blats (as shown below) using Fontographer's drawing tools. Then add the inside text in your page layout application.

Import EPS files

Picture fonts can make great logos, and you can add your own pictures either to an existing picture font, or create your own picture fonts. You can either draw the character right on the screen, or scan it in, or—easiest of all—if you have an EPS file of the graphic, you can simply import the EPS file and it becomes a character. Too cool.

This character was an EPS graphic, originally created in FreeHand.

Design dingbats and borders

Create your own interesting dingbats. Use them as bullets or borders or graphics or graphic elements.

The font inside the border is Fat Freddy Caps from Richard Beatty Designs.

Flip those arrows

Have you ever needed those Zapf Dingbat arrows to point in the other direction? Just open the font, copy them, flip them the way you want, then save them into extra spaces in the font. It would be best to then rename it as a "new" font with these new characters and leave the original Zapf Dingbats intact.

All Zapf Dingbat arrows point to the right, but you can flip them in a split second.

Make bolder or slanted

Have you ever needed your font in a weight that was slightly heavier, but not bold, so you could reverse it? Or did you need it just ever so slightly slanted? Fontographer can take a copy of your whole font and add just the weight or slant you need with the click of a button. (Now, just because you *can* do this doesn't mean you should. A fine typographer who is concerned about the integrity of the typeface would never arbitrarily fatten or slant or contort a classic face. Use this only for decorative pieces or in cases of emergency.)

 *I thickened the strokes just slightly so they would hold up better in the reverse.*

Tilt, skew, flip, rotate, condense

Or you can take as many characters as you choose and flip, rotate, condense, expand, scale, or skew them, or any combination thereof. The gray characters below (as well as the black ones) are actual characters I created and added to the face. They are just typed on the page as you see them.

Acquiring fonts

Type vendors

There are many vendors from whom to purchase fonts. On the next page are the names and addresses of several, but there are hundreds of other vendors, both large and small, with wonderful fonts. So many, in fact, that I am just going to point you to a phenomenal web site that gives you links to every one of them, plus all the new ones that will pop up as soon as this book goes to press.

Prices for typefaces vary considerably, and how you buy fonts also varies. That is, some vendors will only sell an entire family (the entire collection of regular, bold, italic, bold italic, and sometimes even demi and demi-italic) whether you want the whole family or not. Others let you pick and choose a font here and a font there, sometimes with a minimum number.

Fonts on CD-ROM

Several vendors offer their entire collection on a CD-ROM. You buy the CD for a nominal price, and all the fonts on it are locked. You cannot get to a font unless you first pay for the code to unlock it. Once the font is unlocked, you can copy it onto your own hard disk. After you copy it, the original font on the CD is locked again. To get the unlocking code, you simply call the vendor or go to their web site, give them your credit card number, tell them the font you want, and they give you the code over the phone or through e-mail (the code only works once). The advantage to this system is that you have the font instantly.

You can, of course, buy a CD of fonts that are all totally unlocked and available.

Fonts online

Another method of buying commercial or shareware fonts is through the web sites of the font vendors. Using a system similar to the CD-ROM, you can access fonts 24 hours a day by using your credit card number and downloading commercial fonts.

You can also download *freeware* or *shareware* fonts from the web.

What you buy

You don't buy the font itself. What you actually buy is the right, or **license,** to use that font on one *printer*. Often, you must buy a separate license for any additional printers on which you use the font. Check the fine print.

Font vendors

This short list contains just a few of the vendors available. Check the Type Foundry Index web site for a complete and up-to-date list (address is below).

Adobe Systems Inc.
345 Park Avenue
San Jose, CA 95110
408.536.6000
800.445.8787
www.adobe.com/type/

Agfa Direct
90 Industrial Way
Wilmington, MA 01887-1069
800.424.8973
978-658-5600
www.agfahome.com

The Beatty Collection
Hendersonville, NC
704.696.8316

Font Bureau
326 A Street, Suite 6C
Boston, MA 02210
617.423.8770
www.fontbureau.com

FontHaus Inc.
1375 Kings Highway East
Fairfield, CT 06430
800.942.9110
203.367.1993
203.367.1860 fax
www.fonthaus.com

Foster & Horton/FoHo Fonts
211 West Gutierrez Street, #3
Santa Barbara, CA 93101-3481
805.962.3964

GarageFonts
P.O. Box 3101
Del Mar, CA 92014
619.755.4761 phone and fax
www.garagefonts.com

Hoefler Type Foundry, Inc.
611 Broadway, Room 815
New York, NY 10012-2608
212.777.6640
www.typography.com

Image Club Graphics, Inc.
A division of Adobe Systems, Inc.
833 4th Avenue S.W., Suite 800
Calgary, Alberta T2P 3T5
Canada
888.502.8393
403.294.3195
www.imageclub.com

International Typeface Corporation (ITC)
228 East 45th Street, 12th floor
New York, NY 10017
212.949.8072
www.itcfonts.com

LetterPerfect
526 First Avenue South, Suite 227
Seattle, WA 98104
800.929.1951
www.letterspace.com

Plazm Media Cooperative
P.O. Box 2863
Portland, OR 97208-2863
503.222.6389
800.524.4944
www.plazm.com

Web sites you must visit

Chris MacGregor's Internet Type Foundry Index is an incredibly useful site for typophiles. Chris keeps up on who is doing what in the type world and works very hard to maintain this site so it benefits you. He provides a link to every type vendor in the world, plus information on many other aspects of type and a variety of resources. Tell Chris I said hello.

www.typeindex.com

Daniel Will-Harris provides another labor of love, the Will-Harris House, directed to people who care about type. You'll find articles, opinions, humor, and history here. You'll also find an interactive method for determining the most appropriate typeface for a job. Tell Daniel and Toni I said hello.

www.will-harris.com

Vendors of font products

Prices, of course, will change! And the prices might be slightly different depending on whether you buy the software through a catalog, online, or at a store.

Font Management Utilities

Adobe Type Manager Deluxe
$69.99; upgrade $49.99
bundled with Adobe Type
    Reunion Deluxe, $79.99
Adobe Systems, Inc.
345 Park Avenue
San Jose, CA 95110
408.536.6000
800.445.8787
www.adobe.com

Font Reserve $119.95
DiamondSoft, Inc.
351 Jean Street
Mill Valley, CA 94941
415.381.3303
www.fontreserve.com

Suitcase $79.95
Symantec Corporation
175 W. Broadway
Eugene, OR 97401
541.334.6054
800.441.7234
www.symantec.com

MasterJuggler
$49.95; upgrade $29.95
Alsoft, Inc.
P.O. Box 927
Spring, TX 77383
713.353.4090
www.alsoftinc.com

Macromedia Fontographer
600 Townsend Street
San Francisco, CA 94103
415.252.2000
www.macromedia.com

Font Menu Utilities

Adobe Type Reunion (ATR)
$39.99; upgrade $29.99
bundled with
    Adobe Type *Manager* Deluxe,
$79.99
Adobe Systems, Inc.
345 Park Avenue
San Jose, CA 95110
408.536.6000
800.445.8787
www.adobe.com

TypeTamer
$59.95; download a free trial
Impossible Software, Inc.
Irvine, CA 92619-2710
714.479.4800
800.470.4801
www.impossible.com

WYSIWYG Menus
$129.95; upgrade is $29.95
Qualcomm, Inc.
www.nowutilities.com
download a free trial of the
    entire package

MenuFonts
$69.95 retail; $39.95 download
Dubl-Click Software Corporation
20310 Empire Avenue,
    Suite A102
Bend, OR 97701-5713
541.317.0355 voice
541.317.0430 fax
www.dublclick.com *or*
www.unboxed.com

Extra Font Utilities

KeyCap
from Big Rock Software, Inc.,
licensed to Adobe, found on
some Adobe CDs,
such as "Type on Call."

PopChar Lite freeware
PopChar Pro $39 by e-mail;
    $59 on disk
Günter Blaschek
Uni Software Plus GmbH
Softwarepark Hagenberg
Haupstraße 99
A-4232 Hagenberg/Austria
www.unisoft.co.at /products/
popchar.html

*Find the following at
www.shareware.com*

FontView $9 shareware
Simon Brown
211 Banks Street
San Francisco 94110-5624

FontBook $10 shareware
Matthias Kahlert
Haidauer Straße 79
93073 Neutraubling
Germany
mkahlert@kagi,com
www.kagi.com/mkahlert/

FontLoupe $10 shareware
Jonathan
c/o studio format utile
16, rue Baudin
92300 Levallois-Perret
France
format@francenet.fr

Part V

The Glossary

This part contains definitions for the terms you will invariably come across when dealing with fonts and typography. Many of the more complex terms are covered in detail elsewhere in the book, of course. If you don't find quite what you need, try the index to see where else that word is referenced.

Glossary

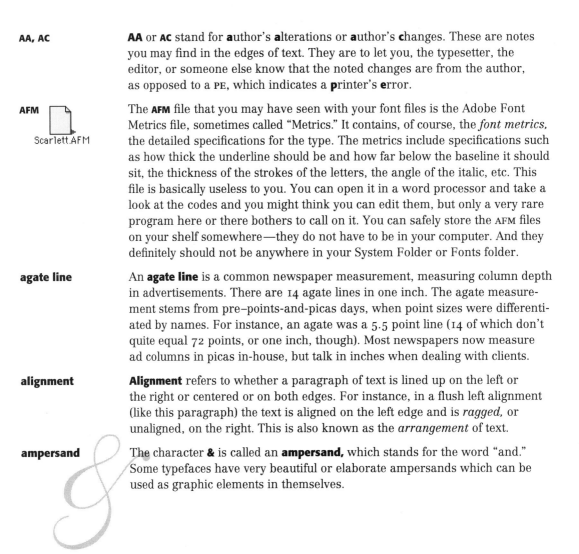

AA, AC

AA or **AC** stand for **a**uthor's **a**lterations or **a**uthor's **c**hanges. These are notes you may find in the edges of text. They are to let you, the typesetter, the editor, or someone else know that the noted changes are from the author, as opposed to a PE, which indicates a **p**rinter's **e**rror.

AFM

Scarlett.AFM

The **AFM** file that you may have seen with your font files is the Adobe Font Metrics file, sometimes called "Metrics." It contains, of course, the *font metrics,* the detailed specifications for the type. The metrics include specifications such as how thick the underline should be and how far below the baseline it should sit, the thickness of the strokes of the letters, the angle of the italic, etc. This file is basically useless to you. You can open it in a word processor and take a look at the codes and you might think you can edit them, but only a very rare program here or there bothers to call on it. You can safely store the AFM files on your shelf somewhere—they do not have to be in your computer. And they definitely should not be anywhere in your System Folder or Fonts folder.

agate line

An **agate line** is a common newspaper measurement, measuring column depth in advertisements. There are 14 agate lines in one inch. The agate measurement stems from pre–points-and-picas days, when point sizes were differentiated by names. For instance, an agate was a 5.5 point line (14 of which don't quite equal 72 points, or one inch, though). Most newspapers now measure ad columns in picas in-house, but talk in inches when dealing with clients.

alignment

Alignment refers to whether a paragraph of text is lined up on the left or the right or centered or on both edges. For instance, in a flush left alignment (like this paragraph) the text is aligned on the left edge and is *ragged,* or unaligned, on the right. This is also known as the *arrangement* of text.

ampersand

The character **&** is called an **ampersand,** which stands for the word "and." Some typefaces have very beautiful or elaborate ampersands which can be used as graphic elements in themselves.

angle bracket

These characters are commonly known as **angle brackets:** < and > . You might also know them as the "greater than" symbol (>) and the "less than" symbol (<). On the keyboard these characters are above the period and the comma. Hold the Shift key down to type them.

apostrophe

This is an **apostrophe:** ' . This is not an apostrophe: ' ; it's a typewriter single quote mark. It's not even a real foot mark.

arrangement

Arrangement refers to whether a paragraph of text is aligned on the left or the right or both or centered or maybe it's not aligned at all. This is also known as *alignment.*

ascender

An **ascender** is the part of some letters that rises above the main body of the letterform. For example, the letters b, d, f, h, and k all have ascenders.

asterisk

This is an **asterisk:** * . The word "asterisk" comes from the Greek word for *star.* It's often called a star instead of an asterisk because so many people can't spell it or pronounce it; it is *not* "ateriks" or "asterik."

asymmetrical

Asymmetrical means it is not even or equal on both sides. If you drew a vertical line through the center of a block of asymmetrically arranged text or an asymmetrically designed page, it would not be exactly the same on both sides of that line.

ATM

ATM stands for Adobe Type Manager, a *utility* that will change your life forever. ATM finds the *printer font* for your typeface and uses it to build the characters on the screen in a very similar way that the printer uses the printer font to put the characters on the page. Thus what you see on the screen is almost as clean as what you know will print. Please see Chapter 7 on Adobe Type Manager for the intimate details.

ATR

ATR stands for Adobe Type Reunion, a little *utility* that cleans up your font menu. See Chapter 13 for more details.

Garamond ▶	Light
Journal	*Light Italic*
Scarlett	Book
Shelley ▶	*Book Italic*
Tekton ▶	*Bold Italic*
	Ultra
	Ultra Italic

This is an example of a menu that uses ATR.

auto kerning

Auto kerning is when a program can take advantage of the "kerning pairs" that are built into a font (see *pair kerning*). Most word processors cannot auto kern, whereas most page layout programs (such as Adobe PageMaker and QuarkXPress) can auto kern. That's one reason why type from a page layout program usually looks so much better than type from a word processor.

baseline

The **baseline** is the invisible line on which type sits.

Oh, regrettable night! ⟵ *This is the baseline*

bitmapped font

A **bitmapped font** is a font that is created and displayed on the screen with pixels (the dots on the screen). The electronic "bits" of information that tell the computer how to display the letters have been "mapped" to the pixels on the screen. Bitmapped fonts are also called *screen fonts.*

Some typefaces are nothing more than bitmapped information, such as most fonts with a city name. Other fonts, like *Type* 1 fonts, have a second part to them, a *printer font,* that is not bitmapped.

What you see on the screen is always bitmapped because that's the only way the screen can display information. But, you say, that's an *outline* font! Well, please read Chapters 3–5 in the Font Technology section to understand the whole picture.

black letter

This is an example of the **black letter** style of type: 𝕱𝖊𝖙𝖙𝖊 𝕱𝖗𝖆𝖐𝖙𝖚𝖗

Black letter types are sometimes called "gothic" (which means "barbaric") or "German blackletter" because the Germans hung on to that style long after the rest of the printing world was using readable type. Sometimes it is mistakenly called "Old English."

bleed

Bleed refers to any element on a page that is printed over the edge of the paper (such as the bar at the top of this page). Whenever you see anything (text, graphics, photographs) that is printed right up to the edge of the paper, it was actually printed *beyond* the margin edge on larger paper, then the paper was trimmed to the size you see. If it was not printed onto larger paper, then the ink would bleed off the paper and onto the press, making a bloody mess.

Some presses might tell you, "No bleeds allowed." Some might say, "We charge extra for bleeds." They might ask, "Does it bleed?" You might say, "Can I bleed this line?"

body

Sometimes the *x-height* of a letterform is known as the **body.** You might say that a particular typeface has a large body. The typeface you are reading right now, called Linotype Centennial at 9 *point,* has a very large body. In fact, at larger sizes it is obnoxious. This is 12-point Centennial.

body clearance

Body clearance is the space above the *ascenders* and below the *descenders* that builds in a little bit of room so the lines of type won't touch each other even if they are *set solid* (meaning with no *leading*). Body clearance is built into the design of the typeface, which is why 30-point type does not really measure 30 points. Also see *x-height.*

Hpxl| *This vertical line is exactly 30 points tall. This typeface is called 30-point type, but it is actually a few points smaller. Those few points allow for the body clearance.*

body copy

On a page of *copy* (text), **body copy** refers specifically to the smaller point size text, the main portion, as opposed to the headlines or the captions. You are reading body copy right now.

bold

Bold type has thicker strokes in the letterforms. It's called "heavier."

This is a light-weight type. **This is a bold, heavy weight.**

bracket (1)

In *typography*, a **bracket** refers to the curve between the *serif* and the stem of a letter. *Oldstyle* typefaces have a prominent, curved bracket. *Modern* typefaces and *slab serif* typefaces have very little or no brackets, or "bracketing."

A bracket ➹ b   *Very little bracketing* ➹ b   *No bracket* ➹ b

bracket (2)

If you're wondering about the characters called **brackets:**
These are square brackets: [ ]
These are curly brackets: { }
These are angle brackets: < > .

bullet

This big round dot is called a **bullet:** •. Press Option 8 in just about any typeface to type a bullet.

cap height

The **cap height** is the height of a typeface's *capital* letters, which are very often shorter than the height of the *ascenders,* as you can see in the example under *body clearance.*

capitals

The "capital," or higher, forms of the letters of our alphabet are known as **capitals** (duh). Capitals are also known as *uppercase, caps,* or (obscurely) as *majuscules.* All writing was done in capital letters for a long time before *lowercase* letters were invented.

caps

Caps is shorthand talk for capital letters. **ALL CAPS** MEANS THE TEXT IS WRITTEN ENTIRELY IN ALL CAPITAL LETTERS, LIKE THIS, WHICH IS MUCH MORE DIFFICULT TO READ.

cdev

A **cdev** is an old term for a Control Panel device (and it's always spelled with lowercase letters). This means it is a little *utility* whose purpose is to make your life easier. For instance, your extra monitor, the number of colors on your monitor, the background pattern of your screen, the view of your Desktop windows, and all kinds of things are controlled, by you, through the various Control Panels.

In System 7 and Mac OS 8, cdevs are called Control Panels and are stored in the Control Panels folder within the System Folder. See *The Little Mac Book* if you need more information on Control Panels or on any other part of the Macintosh operating system.

centered

If type is **centered** (as below), it means the text on each line is centered within the line length. Centered type has symmetrically ragged left and right edges.

"Why, this is so ridiculous!" she cried.
"I must center my life!"

character	A **character** is one single letter, punctuation mark, number, space, etc. Also see the definition for *glyph*.
character set	A **character set** is the entire set of all the single *characters* in the *font*. Every font has the same basic character set that includes capital and lowercase letters, punctuation, and numbers. Some fonts have extra forms in their character set, such as *ligatures* or *dingbats* or alternate *swash* characters. Shown below is the standard character set for *PostScript* or *TrueType* fonts. Use *Key Caps* to see the characters that don't appear on the keyboard.

abcdefghijklmnopqrstuvwxyz   ABCDEFGHIJKLMNOPQRSTUVWXYZ

fiflæœÆŒ   ÅåÂÁÇçÍÎÏÒÓÔØøÚ *(plus you can create just about any accented character)*

ß *f* μ   [ ] ( ) { } < > « » ‹ ›   \ | / /

1234567890 .,;: ... " " ' ' -–—! ? ¡ ¿ •   @ # % ‰ ^ & * ~ _ + = –   ± ÷

™®© $ ¢ £ ¥   § ¶ † ‡ ¬ ª º   ´ ˆ ¨ ˜ ˙ ~ ˘   ˛ ¤ ° · ‚ „ ˝ 1

characters per pica	Before computerized typesetting where we just tweak it 'til it fits, we had to know the **characters per pica** for each size of each typeface so we could calculate how much space the type would take up when typeset. Abbreviated as *cpp,* this is a measurement of how many characters in *that* typeface in *that* size and *that* style using *that* particular typesetting machine would fit in one pica. You can still figure out the characters per pica of any typeface you use on the computer, but why bother.
cicero	A **cicero** is a unit of measure similar to our pica, used in parts of continental Europe. Each cicero has 12 *didot* points, or "corps." One American/English pica is .167 of an inch; one cicero is .177 of an inch.
city-named fonts	A **city-named font** is a font called by a city name, such as Geneva, New York, Boston, or Cairo. Traditionally on the Macintosh the non–*TrueType* city-named fonts are *bitmapped fonts* that have no *printer font* to match. They are designed around the limitations of the resolution of the screen, 72 dots per inch, so on the screen a city-named font is actually easier to read than a non–city-named font. When you print to a low-resolution printer such as the ImageWriter, they also appear easier to read.

There are a few city-named fonts that were named after a city before the Macintosh was invented, fonts such as Memphis or Alexandria. These are real fonts, not bitmapped ones designed for low resolution. How do you know which ones are which? If they came with your Mac, they are TrueType or bitmapped. |
| **Clarendon** | **Clarendon** is the name of a type family in the *slab serif* category. It is such a perfect example of a slab serif that sometimes people call that entire category of type "Clarendons." The font New Century Schoolbook, which is probably on your computer, is a slab serif. Also see *Egyptian*. |

cold type   Not very long ago, into the 1970s in many places, type was always set with *hot metal.* Literally, hot molten lead was poured into little molds of letterforms. These were inked and pressed onto paper to create a proof, or a printed page. The designer used these proofs to paste up their final designed pages. Whole pages were made of metal type to print books, magazines, and newspapers. Well, the type we have now is obviously no longer hot metal and so is known as **cold type.** This was a particularly important distinction when the technology was going through the first transition from hot metal to phototypesetting.

color   **Color** in typography does not refer to the colors we usually think of. It refers to the overall tone, density, and texture of a page of type in black and white. You usually want an even color on the page. The color is influenced by the size of the type, the style, the thickness of the strokes, the contrast or lack of contrast between the thick-and-thin parts of the strokes, the space between the letters, the lines, and the words, the amount of open space in the *counters,* and a few other factors.

complex family   Please see *family,* and also see the little chart on page 15.

composition   The act of setting type, of *typesetting,* is often called **composition.** Newspapers had whole entire composition rooms, or composing rooms, where men (almost always men) would put those little metal lines of type together into pages of type.

condensed   A typeface that is **condensed** is one that has been designed with a narrower than normal width. Please also see *set width.*

This is normal. This is a condensed version of the same face. This is extra condensed.

copy   **Copy,** in a type sense, means the text itself. It used to mean the typewritten text before it was typeset, but now so much text goes straight to the screen that often all text is considered to be copy.

copyfitting   **Copyfitting** is the process of taking type**written** (or handscrawled) *copy* and determining how much space the finished type**set** text will occupy. It involves counting the number of characters, looking up the *cpp,* measuring the available space, and performing wonderful algebraic equations to see if the font in the size and style you wanted would fit in the space. Not many people spend the time to copyfit anymore, since you can now do it on the screen right in front of your face.

counter   A **counter** is the white space inside a letterform, those holes you fill in when you're talking on the phone. It includes the space inside of **o** and **p,** as well as the open forms as in the letter **c** or the bottom portion of the **e** or in a capital **G.** The size and openness of the counters in a typeface influence its *readability, legibility,* and *color.*

cpp   See *characters per pica.*

curly quotes	**Curly quotes** is a descriptive term for real quotation marks ("") as opposed to typewriter quotation marks (", also known as "straight quotes" or "dumb quotes"). Real quotation marks curl toward the words, as shown below. They are sometimes known as "sixes and nines," since the opening quotes look like number sixes, and the closing quotes look like number nines.

"She wrapped herself in an enigma."

cursive	**Cursive** refers to letterforms based on calligraphy or handwriting. Sometimes "kursive" is applied to *sans serif* type that has been merely slanted, rather than entirely redesigned as an *italic* typeface.
decorative	A **decorative** typeface is one that is too fancy to read very well in body copy—often it's too fancy for anything but a couple of words, as in a masthead or logotype. Decorative faces often evoke a particular response, which is their strength. They usually need to be set in larger sizes.

THIS IS DEFINITELY DECORATIVE.

descender	A **descender** is the part of some letters (such as p, y, or g) that descends below the *baseline,* which is the invisible line that type sits on.
desktop publishing	**Desktop publishing** (also known as DTP) is the use of a personal computer to create (publish) pages that contain text and graphics. It's considered "desktop" publishing as a distinction from the graphic design or advertising studio or the typesetting shop, which used to be the only places that knew how to create finished pages. Now everyone with a desk or even a lap can publish newsletters, flyers, package design, books, web pages, etc.
didot point	A **didot point** is a unit of measure similar to our *point,* used in parts of continental Europe. Twelve *didot* points, or "corps," makes one *cicero,* similar to our *pica.* One American/English pica is .167 of an inch; one cicero is .177 of an inch.
dingbat	Cute as this word is, **dingbat** is actually a traditional printers' term identifying those little decorative elements, decorations like stars and hearts and tiny flowers and snowflakes. These are dingbats: ★✐✳✄➤✳☐✳✂✳✿■
discretionary hyphen	A **discretionary hyphen,** affectionately known as a "dischy," is a hyphen you can type to hyphenate a word at the end of a line. Then if you edit the text in any way so that the hyphenated word is no longer at the end of the line, the discretionary hyphen just disappears (rather than appear in the middle of the word in the middle of the sentence, as a regular hyphen would). The discretionary hyphen will appear again at the end of a line if necessary.
	In both QuarkXPress and PageMaker you can type a discretionary hyphen by pressing Command Hyphen or Command Shift Hyphen (depending on your version). Also see *non-breaking characters.*

display initial   See *initial cap.*

display type   **Display type** refers to type over the size of 14 point, such as headlines. In some *expert sets,* a font has been redesigned as a "display" font. This means it has been redesigned specifically for larger sizes, usually over 24 point, with thinner strokes, a slightly different proportion of x-height to cap height, adjustments to where the curves meet the stems, more delicate serifs, etc.

dots per inch   **Dots per inch** is how we measure the *resolution* of a printer. The higher the number of dots per inch, the higher the resolution, and the more clearly the text or image can be displayed or printed.

The resolution of monitors is not measured by the number of dots per inch, but by the range, determined by the bit depth, of the pixels.

doubling   When you try to read the next line of type in a paragraph but you find you read the first line over again, that is called **doubling.** It often happens if the line length is too long or if the space between the lines is too tight.

downloadable font   A **downloadable font** is a font that is not *resident* in your printer; that is, it does not live in the memory of your printer. If you have acquired *PostScript* or *TrueType* fonts from anywhere, they are downloadable fonts. When you print with them, the computer must download the fonts, or load them down into, the printer. Please see the detailed information in Chapter 5 on PostScript fonts.

dpi   The acronym **dpi** stands for *dots per inch.*

drop cap   See *initial cap.*

drop-out type   **Drop-out type** is type that is removed from an image so the background paper color shows through. Usually drop-out type drops out of some sort of graphic, whereas *reverse type* is taken out of a solid color.

Drop out this type.   Reverse this type.

DTP   **DTP** is an abbreviation for *desktop publishing.*

dumb apostrophe   A **dumb apostrophe**, a fake one, a straight one, a typewriter apostrophe, looks like this: '. A smart apostrophe looks like this: ' .

dumb quote   A **dumb quote,** a fake one, a straight one, a typewriter quotation mark, looks like this: " ". Smart quotes (curly quotes) look like this: " ".

Dvorak keyboard   **Dvorak** is the name of a **keyboard** arrangement of characters that is much more efficient than our present standard *Qwerty* arrangement. The letters are in different places; the different positions take advantage of our stronger fingers. Typing speed can be increased dramatically and with less trauma to the hands. There is software you can install in your computer that will let your keyboard use the Dvorak arrangement. Please also see *Qwerty.*

Egyptian type　　**Egyptian** is the name sometimes given to the *slab serif* category of type. This category was becoming popular just as the Rosetta Stone unlocked the key to Egyptian mysteries and the world went through an Egyptomania phase. Thus many of the slab serifs designed during this period were named with Egyptian names just so they would be popular, faces like Scarab, Memphis, Alexandria, Cairo, Pyramid. A more accurate name for this category is *Clarendon*.

elite　　**Elite** is any *monospaced* typewriter face that sets 12 characters per inch, which is called its "pitch." *Pica* is a similar face that sets 10 characters per inch, so it's called 10-pitch. IBM computers still use these primitive faces.

ellipsis, ellipses　　The **ellipsis** character is the three dots: … ("ellipses" is plural). You can type an ellipsis by pressing Option ; (semicolon). It's handy occasionally, particularly because your word processing or page layout program won't end a line between the ellipsis dots.

For fine typography, though, it is preferable that you create your own ellipsis with a space dot space. To prevent the three dots from separating onto two lines if they land at the end of a line, use a *non-breaking space* such as an *en space* or a *thin space* between the dots.

em, en, thin　　An **em** is a measurement that is the width of the point size of the type. For instance, if you are using 12 point type, an em (whether it is an *em space* or an *em dash*) will be 12 points wide. An em is approximately the size of a capital letter M in that typeface (although it has nothing at all to do with the letter M). Typesetters used to call an em a "mutton" to distinguish it from an *en*.

An **en** is half the width of an em and was sometimes called a "nut." An en is approximately the size of a capital letter N in that typeface.

A **thin** is one-fourth the width of an em.

em dash　　An **em dash** is the name of the long dash used in professional type, as opposed to the two hyphens that we used on a typewriter because we didn't have a long dash character.

To type an em dash (—), press Option Shift Hyphen.

em space　　An **em space** is a *non-breaking* space that is the width of an *em*. The standard indent for paragraphs is one em space (not five spaces or one-half inch, as you were taught on your typewriter).

en dash　　An **en dash** is the name of the middle-sized dash used in professional type. On a typewriter you probably used a hyphen for it. The grammatical place to use an en dash is wherever you have been sticking a hyphen instead of the word "to" or "through." For instance, these phrases should have an en dash, not a hyphen: 5–7 years; 10:30–12 noon; New York–Chicago flight. Also use it when you need to hyphenate a word that is already more than two words long, like "pre–points and picas."

To type an en dash (–), press Option Hyphen.

en space

An **en space** is a *non-breaking* space that is the width of an *en*. An en (as noted on the previous page) is a space about the width of a capital letter N.

expert sets

An **expert set,** or **expert collection,** is a font that has more refined typographic characters than most other fonts. An expert set usually has more *ligatures* than a regular font, plus proportionally correct *small caps, oldstyle figures,* and perhaps some well-designed *swash* characters. If you're lucky you'll get a *display* set. At this point in time, expert sets can be a pain in the neck to use because of all the options, but you really do need an expert set when you want to create very fine and extremely high-quality typography.

extended font

An **extended font** is a typeface designed to appear wide and stretched.

This is regular. These characters are extended.

extended text

Extended text means a lot of text that is meant for long periods of reading, as in a book or long brochure or annual report, as opposed to a short block or two of text in an advertisement.

extension

An **extension** is a little program that does things like make extra sounds, pictures, clocks, etc., or helps run your computer. Older versions of the font management programs *Suitcase* and *MasterJuggler* are extensions. Store extensions in the Extensions folder inside the System Folder; they won't work if you put them anywhere else.

family

A **family** of type contains all the related fonts with the same design characteristics (and the same name). For instance, Garamond, Garamond Bold, Garamond Italic, Garamond Bold Italic, Garamond Condensed, and Garamond Ultra Condensed are all part of the same family.

With computer font technology, families have become either *simple* or *complex*. A **simple family** is one that has just four styles (regular, italic, bold, bold italic). A **complex family** is one that has more variations, such as semibold, extended, condensed, ultra condensed, etc. These distinctions become important when you start trying to manage a large number of fonts.

first-line indent

A **first-line indent** is when the first line of a paragraph is indented. On a typewriter you had to set a tab stop and hit the Tab key at the beginning of each paragraph. But just about every program on the Mac that sets words lets you set a first-line indent stop. Then every time you hit the Return key, the Mac knows the next line is the first line of the next paragraph and indents it automatically. If you choose to indent your paragraphs, you really ***must*** learn how to use the first-line indent feature. Too bad my little book, *Tabs and Indents on the Macintosh* (clever title) is out of print.

fit

The **fit** of type refers to the spacing between the letters and whether the spacing is tight, normal, loose, very loose, or very tight. It also refers to the visual consistency of the letter spacing; the ideal is an appearance of an even, consistent amount of space between all the letters.

flush left

Flush left is a typographic arrangement where the text is aligned on the left side and is *ragged,* or not aligned, on the right. Flush left text is the easiest to read because the word spacing is always consistent, plus the eye always knows where the beginning of the line is. The text on these pages is set flush left.

flush right

Flush right is a typographic arrangement where the text is aligned on the right side and is *ragged,* or not aligned, on the left. It makes a nice effect sometimes, but keep in mind that it is not easy to read over a period of time because your eye always has to look for the beginning of the next line. Also see *alignment.*

.fog

Scarlett.fog

A file with a **.fog** at the end of its name is a Fontographer database file. This is where Fontographer keeps all the information while you build the typeface in the program. If you want to edit a font, you can open and use the .fog file, or you can open the outline file of the font if it's finished.

folio

Folio means page number, as in, "I think the folio should be on the bottom of the page rather than on the side."

FOND

FOND is a special resource that stands for Font Family Descriptor. It holds information about a specific *family* of type, such as the Garamond family.

font ID conflict

A **font ID conflict** is when your fonts get confused about who they are. It can happen easily when you create a document on your computer and then take it to someone else's computer. When it was on your machine the font was, say, Bembo. But when you take it to your friend's machine, it gets confused and thinks it is Korinna. It can even happen on your own computer, where you choose the font Janson and the font Souvenir shows up. See Chapter 14.

font ID number

Every font is identified within the Mac by a particular number, the **font ID number.** The method of identification has changed over the years and is still not quite perfected, which is why there are still *font ID conflicts.* See Chapter 14.

font management

Font management is the process of controlling your fonts so your fonts always appear on the screen properly, print properly, are easy to find, and are easy to gather for output to a service bureau. See Part III on Font Management.

font metrics

The **font metrics** (which can be read in an *AFM* file) are all the specifications for a typeface, including how thick the underline should be, the width of the characters, the thickness of the strokes, the size of the capital letters, etc.

format

When you **format** text, it means you apply certain characteristics to the words on the page. You choose a font, a type size, and a style such as italic or regular. Perhaps you adjust the letterspacing or the word spacing. Maybe you set up some tabs. After these kinds of changes, you have formatted text.

fraction bar

The **fraction bar** may look like a slash but it is actually a different character. The fraction bar is bent at a different angle to accommodate the fraction, and it does not descend below the *baseline.* And the fraction bar is a *non-breaking character,* meaning the computer cannot break the fraction at the end of a line: that is, if the fraction ¾ is separated by a regular slash bar, you could potentially end up with the ³⁄ at the end of a line and the ₄ at the beginning of the next line. If you use the fraction bar, the characters in ¾ will never be separated from each other. To type the fraction bar, press Option Shift 1.

This is the slash: _____ /

This is the fraction bar: ___ /

galley
A **galley** is a proof, or a final draft, of the finished set type, usually used for approval by the client before final prodution. All type used to come back from the typesetters in galleys—your entire newsletter would be on a strip of resin-coated paper about four or five feet long. You had to cut out the stories and the headlines with a knife and paste them onto the illustration board. Oh, don't you miss those days? Ask someone who used to do this how they fixed a typo under a tight deadline. Ha! That's when I discovered I should have been an eye surgeon.

glyph
A **glyph** is kind of like a *character,* but more generic; a character is what you type, but a glyph is what you see. The word glyph easily covers any letter of the alphabet, any number, accent mark, dingbat, swash, foreign character—any printable image that can be mapped to the keyboard.

gutter
A **gutter** is the space between two columns of type. A gutter is also the space between two pages where they are bound together.

hairline (1)
A **hairline** is a very thin *rule,* or line. Technically, it is supposed to be ¼ *point.* On a laser printer a hairline cannot print as thin as it is supposed to be, but on an *imagesetter* those same hairlines are incredibly thin. Be careful if you are going to *output* to an imagesetter, because hairlines can be difficult for a press to reproduce. This is a hairline: _____

hairline (2)
A **hairline** also refers to the thinnest strokes of a letterform. You might hear someone say, "These hairlines in this reverse type are going to disappear," meaning the thin strokes are going to clog up with ink and they won't print very well.

hanging indent
A **hanging indent** (also known as an *outdent*) is when the first line begins to the left of the rest of the paragraph. All of the definitions in this glossary are set up in a hanging indent form. Numbered lists are generally set with a hanging indent. If you don't know how to use your indents, you really should have read my little book *Tabs and Indents,* but it's out of print now.

This paragraph is indented.
This was only one of the signs of her coming dementia; her delusions became progressively more literary and bizarre.

This paragraph has a hanging indent.
This was only one of the signs of her coming dementia; her delusions became progressively more literary and bizarre.

Examples written by Karen Elizabeth Gordon, from The Well-Tempered Sentence.

This list uses a hanging indent to hang the numbers off to the left.

1. As a rule I hate iguanas, but this one had a wistful face.
2. Who was it who wrote, "Life is a stage attacked by an idiot"?

155

hang,
hanging punctuation
When a quotation mark is on the left edge of aligned type, or when almost any punctuation is at the right edge of aligned type, it often creates the appearance of an indent where there isn't supposed to be one. To keep the edges of type visually aligned, often it is necessary to **hang the punctuation;** that is, to move the punctuation mark beyond the edge of the aligned text. There are various ways to do this, depending on the program.

"It was a
grand adventure.
I am content."

W.A. Dwiggins
_____

*The quote mark makes
the first line appear to
be indented, wouldn't
you agree?*

"It was a
grand adventure.
I am content."

W.A. Dwiggins
_____

*Now the quote mark is
hanging off the edge of
the left indent. Doesn't
this look so much better?*

hard copy
Hard copy is the copy of your document that comes out of the printer. "Hard" means you can touch it.

hard space
A **hard space** is a space that does not "break"; it's a space that the computer thinks is a regular character as if it were in a word. For instance, when you type a regular space between Ms. and Boadicea and the word Ms. gets to the end of a line, the line will break there and Boadicea will move to the next line. But if you put a hard space between Ms. and Boadicea, the two words will never be separated. Most programs will give you a hard space the size of a regular word space if you press Option Spacebar. Hard spaces are also known as *non-breaking spaces.* Other hard spaces are the *em space, en space,* and *thin space.*

headline
Headline refers to the main title of a portion of text. It is usually bigger in size than the *body copy* and is often bold or in a different font.

Helvetica Narrow
You may find **Helvetica Narrow** on your computer pretending to be a condensed (narrower) version of Helvetica. But it is not a *true-drawn* face—it is a fake. The Mac just takes Helvetica and squishes it for you. This is okay if you are just going to print directly to your own laser printer, but if you try to print Helvetica Narrow to an *imagesetter* you will probably get poorly spaced Courier instead. If you really want a condensed Helvetica (though I can't imagine why you'd want to use *any* sort of Helvetica), you really should invest in a true-drawn font.

hinting
The **hinting** adjusts the letterforms when they are printed at small sizes on lower resolution machines (lower resolution such as 300 or 600 *dpi,* like your laser printer), as well as on the screen, so the letters are sharper and clearer.

hot type

Hot type, also called "hot metal," refers to the kind of type that was state-of-the-art from the mid-1500s until the 1970s (oh, some would complain that hot type was gone before then, but it was common until the mid-seventies and is still found in parts of the world). All type used to be made out of hot metal—literally hot, molten lead. The melted lead was poured into little molds, cooled, and pages were printed from the raised letters (well, that's the *basic* idea). Then the metal letters were melted down again and the lead was re-used. With the advent of phototypesetting in the '70s, the term *cold type* was created to distinguish the technologies.

icon

An **icon,** in computer jargon, is a little picture that represents data (information) that is stored in your computer, or it symbolizes the function it will do.

ID conflict, ID number

See *font id conflict.*

imagesetter

An **imagesetter** is just a bigger printer than yours. Well, it's really big, like about $100,000 big. Shops that invest in imagesetters and provide the *output* service to people are called *service bureaus.* You take your disk (the same disk you used to print your document at home) to a service bureau; they put your disk into their Mac and output (print) your document—instead of to a laser printer—to a *high-resolution* imagesetter. The document comes out on photo-sensitive paper, which is smooth and thicker than plain paper. Your laser printer probably prints at 300 to 600 *dots per inch.* An imagesetter prints from 1,270 to 2,540 dots per inch.

initial cap

An **initial cap** is a letter, usually the first letter in a paragraph, that is larger and often more elaborate than the rest of the text. Its purpose is decorative. Initial caps are also known as "drop caps" or "decorative caps."

One important design decision with initial caps: please make sure the bottom of the initial letter is aligned with a *baseline!*

The "L" is an initial cap.

Love is like war: easy to begin but very hard to stop.

—H.L. Mencken

installed size

If you are not using *ATM (Adobe Type Manager)* and if you are not using *TrueType* (don't worry if you don't know whether you are or not) then you will notice that some sizes look smoother than others; for instance, 14 point looks much better than 16 point. This is because certain sizes of fonts (also called "fixed-size bitmaps") have been **installed** in your system, and the computer then knows how to build that size. If you ask for a size that is not installed, the Mac has to figure out how to build it and it always looks crummy. See the illustrations and the in-depth explanations in Chapter 3.

italic

Italic is a style variation of a typeface: *this is italic.* You know what it is. A real italic is *true-drawn;* that is, the designer redrew the letterforms in the italic version, as opposed to the computer taking the *roman* version and just slanting it. Notice the completely different letterforms between the roman word and the true-drawn italic words below, particularly the g, a, and f:

giraffe   *giraffe*

Some typefaces have just been slanted, using a computer command. This is not really italic, but merely skewed, or at best, *oblique.*

giraffe   *giraffe*

justified

Justified type is text that is aligned on both sides of the column, as in this paragraph. The computer justifies the text by adding or deleting space between the words on each line to force the words to fit. If there are not enough words on a line, you'll get big gaps between words. If the words cannot be hyphenated, you'll get lines with words all smished together.

Only justify your type if the line length is long enough to avoid awkward word spacing. A good rule of thumb is to justify type only if the line length in *picas* is at least twice the *point* size of the type. That is, if you are using 12 point type, the line length should be at least 24 picas before you justify (there are 6 picas in 1 inch). From that basic rule, then consider the typeface, the purpose, etc., to determine whether it is appropriate and feasible to justify.

kerning

Kerning is the process of adjusting the space between letters so the spacing appears to be visually consistent. Certain letter combinations, such as **Ta** or **Vo** naturally have too much space between them, and a designer or typographer must manually adjust the spacing so it matches the rest of the text.

Key Caps

Key Caps is a desk accessory where you can find all the alternate characters, such as ©, ®, ™, or ¢ in the font of your choice. Please see brief instructions on how to use Key Caps on page 121, or explicit directions in *The Little Mac Book* or *The Mac is not a typewriter.*

keyboard layout

One definition of a **keyboard layout** is the arrangement of the keys. The standard layout is called *qwerty* because of the first six letters across the alphabetic row on your keyboard.

The Qwerty layout was purposefully created to be inefficient. The mechanical keyboards of the late 1800s jammed easily because the typists' fingers could move faster than the keys, so a typewriter designer, C.L. Sholes, arranged the characters in such a way as to slow down the typist.

The *Dvorak* layout has a very different keyboard arrangement, one that is supposed to be incredibly more efficient than the Qwerty. Just about any personal computer can be switched to understand the Dvorak layout.

The *Maltron keyboard* refers to a different shape of keyboard, which can use either a Qwerty or Dvorak layout.

keyboard mapping

Keyboard mapping refers to the way the characters are "mapped" to the keyboard you use; that is, what characters will appear when you press a certain key or combination of keys. Most typefaces have a pretty standard map of the regular characters and numbers. Then depending on what *font* (typeface) you are using, and particularly depending on what kind of computer you are using, there may be other keyboard maps with alternate characters for each typeface.

LaserWriter 35

The LaserWriter 35 are the 35 *PostScript* fonts that are *resident* in the Apple LaserWriters. They include Avant Garde, Bookman, Helvetica, New Century Schoolbook, Palatino, Times, Symbol, Zapf Chancery, Zapf Dingbats, and Courier, along with their attendant italics, bolds, and bold italics.

lc, l.c.

The letters **lc** stand for *lowercase*.

leading

Leading (pronounced *ledding*) is the amount of space between lines of text. The term comes from the little strips of lead that used to be inserted between the lines when all type was made of metal.

There are 72 points in one inch. Most of the text you read is in 9, 10, 11, or 12 point type. Leading adds a few *points* of space between the lines. So if leading is just a few points, why do you choose amounts like 12, 14, and 18 point leading? Well, it works this way: you take the point size of your type, say 12 point. You add a couple points of lead, say 3 points. You add the 12 and the 3 together and we say you have a leading value of 15.

one line of 12-point type

second line of 12-point type

The type is 12 point, the leading is 3 point. The total leading value is considered 15 point.

A standard amount of leading is 20 percent of the point size of the type. That is, if your type is 10 point, the standard amount of leading to add is 2 points. This is the norm from which you can deviate, depending on whether you want tight lines, loose lines, if your type has a large *x-height* or a small one, whether you're trying to conserve space or fill it, whether your type is bold and black or light and airy, etc.

It is entirely possible to have *negative leading,* where the leading value is less than the point size of the type. This is very common with large type, especially when there aren't many *descenders.*

Kumquat Meringue

This example is 30-point type with 24-point lead, which is actually –6 points of leading, right?

The term "leading" was just being phased out for the more appropriate term "linespacing" (since we no longer use lead) when *desktop publishing* hit the streets and hung onto the outdated term "leading." Now it looks as though we're stuck with "leading" for a while longer.

legibility

Legibility is different from *readability*. Legibility refers to how easily individual letterforms can be distinguished one from another; for instance, how quickly you can distinguish an "n" from an "h." Readability refers to how easily a lot of text can be read without tiring your eyes or driving you nuts.

There have been extensive studies on legibility and readability. The studies show that *sans serif* typefaces are more *legible* than *serif* typefaces. That is, it is easier to instantly recognize a short burst of text set in a sans serif font. (Serif type, on the other hand, is more **readable;** it is much easier to read large amounts of text set in a serif face.) Now, this doesn't mean that every sans serif is legible. There are many design features that create or destroy legibility. See my book, *Beyond The Mac is not a typewriter.*

letter fit

Traditionally, *kerning* has meant to decrease the amount of space between pairs of letters. When space was added between pairs of letters, it was known as **letter fit.** Now, like the term kerning, letter fit simply refers to the visually consistent spacing between letters. Also see *fit.*

letterspacing

Letterspacing refers to the overall space between the letters. *Kerning* is a matter of adjusting the space between two specific characters.

THIS TEXT IS LETTERSPACED

When people say that text is "letterspaced," though, it has a more specific meaning: it means there is intentionally extra space between the letters. Some typographers feel it is a great sin to letterspace lowercase letters because Frederic Goudy, a great typographer, once said "Anyone who would letterspace lowercase letters would steal sheep." (He was actually talking about letterspacing *black letter.*) Personally, I don't find letterspaced lowercase letters to be terribly offensive.

ligature

A **ligature** is one character that is really two characters combined into one, usually created to solve a spacing or design problem. For instance, when a lowercase "i" is next to a lowercase "f," the hook of the "f" often bumps into the dot of the "i." So a ligature was created to make the "f" and the "i" one character. Some fonts have other ligatures for the character combinations "fl," "ffl," "ffi," "oe," "st," etc.

Without ligatures: fireflight   *With ligatures:* fireflight

To type the fi ligature: press **Shift Option 5**
To type the fl ligature: press **Shift Option 6**
To type other ligatures, you need a font that has been designed with the characters. *Expert sets* usually have more ligatures available.

linespacing

Linespacing is the space between the lines of type, which you may also hear referred to as *leading.* It was properly termed "leading" when all type was made out of molten lead, but "linespacing" is really a more appropriate term at this point in history. Unfortunately the computers don't always follow typographic trends (as evidenced by the fact that every one of them arrives with Helvetica installed). Please see *leading.*

lining figures

Lining figures are the numbers you are used to typing. They all line up on the *baseline* and they all take up the same amount of space; that is, the number "1" takes up as much space as the number "8" (they are *monospaced*). Lining figures have to be monospaced so they will line up in columns. Compare lining figures with *oldstyle figures.*

Lino

Lino is an affectionate term for the Linotronic brand of *imagesetters.* The word "lino" is often used like we use the words "Kleenex" or "Xerox"—a trade name used as a generic term to mean anything similar. You might say, "I'm going to lino this," or "Take this to lino," or "Lino [meaning the *output*] is so pretty."

lowercase

Lowercase refers to the small letters of our alphabet, also known as *minuscules* or *lc.* See *uppercase* for the interesting story of where we get the words lower- and uppercase.

majuscules

Majuscules is an old calligraphic term for capital letters. *Minuscules* is the companion term for *lowercase* letters.

Maltron

The **Maltron keyboard** has a different shape from the standard, familiar, rectangular board. The Maltron keyboard is designed to prevent stress on your hands. The keys are laid out in two concave areas conforming to the shape of hands, which minimizes long finger stretches and keeps the forearms aligned with the wrists. It's less tiring to use because the most-often used characters are situated under the strongest fingers, including up to eight keys for each thumb (although a Maltron keyboard *can* be set up in the standard *Qwerty* layout if you choose).

mark-up

To **mark-up** means to take your pen (aack—you mean manually?) and write typesetting specifications all over the page. We no longer have to mark-up typewritten copy (usually), but we still mark-up computer-generated copy for improvements.

merge

Do the various members of a font *family* show up in your menu scattered all over the place? Is Garamond Bold alphabetized under "B Garamond Bold," and Garamond Italic under "I Garamond Italic"? And if you want to italicize Garamond, do you have to choose the font "I Garamond Italic" instead of hitting the keyboard shortcut? Well, if a font family is **merged,** it means the family members have been combined into one neat little unit; the family name Garamond will appear in the menu once, and you can use keyboard shortcuts to access the italic, bold, etc.

*Adobe Type Reunion makes submenus for family members (as in Garamond). **Merging** the font family leaves one name in the menu (as in Helvetica or Palatino) that represents all the styles.*

Some font vendors have merged the families for you already. The font utility *Suitcase* has a separate little utility that can merge families for you, if you like, but I don't recommend it. If you do merge your own families, be conscious when you take your file that uses merged fonts to a *service bureau*—you should also take a font ID file with you. See Chapter 14 on font ID conflicts.

metrics	See _font metrics._
minus linespacing	See _negative leading._
minuscules	**Minuscules** is an old calligraphic term for _lowercase_ letters. _Majuscules_ is the companion term for _capital_ letters.
modern	**Modern** is a category of typeface that has thin horizontal _serifs_ and a radical contrast between the thick and thin parts of the strokes.

This is Poster Bodoni Compressed, an example of a modern type.

monospace	If a typeface is **monospaced,** like this paragraph, it means each character in the font takes up the same amount of space as any other. For instance, the letter i or even a period takes up the same width of space as a capital W. You can actually draw lines to separate the columns of type. Almost all typewriter fonts were monospaced. Using a monospaced font today makes your work look outdated and unprofessional.
Multiple Masters	**Multiple Masters** is a font technology that allows you to create new fonts based on an existing font, changing the width and thickness of the characters in infinite varieties to suit your needs—with only the click of a button. It is a fascinating and valuable technology. See another book of mine for details, _The Non-Designer's Type Book._
negative leading, minus leading, minus linespacing	First of all, a _leading_ measurement is the point size of the type _plus_ the number of points that are added between the lines of text. For instance, 24 point type with 6 points of lead (space) between the lines makes what we call 30 point leading. It is written 24/30 (pronounced 24 on 30). When there is no extra space added between the lines, it is called _set solid_, such as 24/24 (pronounced 24 on 24 or just called "solid").

With phototype and computer type such as you use right now, it is possible to have leading values like this: 24/20. This is **negative leading** because the amount of leading added to the point size of the type is –4.

It's very common (and usually desirable) to have negative leading in larger point sizes, and it's almost imperative to have negative leading when a line is all caps or there are no characters with descenders.

Far From the Madding Crowd

This title is 36-point type with a leading value of 24, which actually makes a negative leading of –12.

NFNT

After realizing that the original FONT identification system for numbering fonts was much too limited to be adequate, Apple developed a new kind of identification structure called **NFNT** (for "new font," pronounced *en font* or sometimes just n-f-n-t). It allows for about 16,000 ID numbers for fonts, which helped resolve the *font ID conflicts.*

non-breaking characters

Non-breaking characters are characters that the software program cannot hyphenate at the end of a line. For instance, if you make a fraction with the regular slash bar, it is possible to have the top half of the fraction at the end of one line and the bottom half at the beginning of the next line. But if you use the non-breaking *fraction bar,* the top and bottom halves can never be separated. Type the fraction bar by pressing Option Shift 1.

There is also a non-breaking hyphen. In PageMaker, type it by pressing Command Option Hyphen. In QuarkXPress type it by pressing Command Equal (=).

If your program has a *discretionary hyphen,* you can type that hyphen in front of any word to prevent the word from breaking. The discretionary hyphen does not appear on the screen or in your text.

Also see *non-breaking spaces.*

non-breaking spaces

Non-breaking spaces are blank spaces of varying widths. Unlike a typical Spacebar word space, a non-breaking space is "hard," meaning the computer thinks it is a character, not a space between words. Two words separated by a non-breaking space of any sort will not break; that is, the two words will never separate onto two different lines. For instance, if you're writing about the Mach II airplane, you probably don't want the II to end up on the next line all by itself, separated from Mach. So instead of typing a regular space between the words, type a hard space. The computer will then think Mach II is one word, and since it can't find that word in its dictionary, it can never be separated.

In just about every program you can type Option Spacebar (instead of the regular Spacebar) to create a hard, non-breaking space that is usually the same size as the Spacebar word space. Some programs have an *em space,* an *en space,* and/or a *thin space* as well.

oblique

Oblique in typography refers to slanted type, as opposed to *italic* type. Typically, an oblique look has been applied by the computer, as opposed to italic, in which the letterforms have been redesigned by the designer. It is typographically gauche to oblique type that shouldn't be oblique; that is, unless you have a good reason (like you want to freak out a traditional typographer), don't use the keyboard commands to oblique or slant your text.

roman   *true italic*   *obliqued roman*

Many sans serif faces have, instead of an italic version, an oblique version of the face included in the family. This may have been designed into the typeface or it may have been computer-generated. The standard slant is 12 degrees.

oldstyle

Oldstyle refers to a category of type designed on the principles of the original typefaces that were cast in the 16ᵀᴴ century. Oldstyle type has slanted *serifs,* a gradual *thick-thin* transition, and a decidely diagonal *stress.*

This is an oldstyle face, Garamond.

oldstyle figures

Oldstyle figures are numbers that are designed to emulate the *lowercase* look of type, with *ascenders* and *descenders:* 1234567890 (lining figures) *vs.* 1234567890 (oldstyle figures). Oldstyle figures blend into a line of type much more smoothly than do *lining figures,* which call too much attention to themselves—they are like setting a word in all caps. Once you work with oldstyle figures it is hard to go back to lining figures. Oldstyle figures are typically only found in *expert set* fonts. I use oldstyle figures in this book.

6275 Sunset Lane, Suite 389   **6275 Sunset Lane, Suite 389**
Magdalena, New Mexico 87825   **Magdalena, New Mexico 87825**

orphan

There is and always has been and probably always will be quibbling about the exact meaning of an **orphan.** I define an orphan as the last line of a paragraph alone at the top of the next column, or the first line of a paragraph alone at the bottom of a column. Some people call this typographic faux pas a *widow.* It doesn't matter what you call it—don't do it. Also see *widow.*

outdent

An *outdent* is when the first line of a paragraph starts to the left of the rest of the text. This is the same as a *hanging indent,* and is the opposite of a *first-line indent.* Please see the illustration under *hanging indent.*

outline font

An **outline font,** sometimes called a *printer font,* is actually a mathematical formula that tells the printer how to create a particular typeface. Because of this mathematical outline (rather than simple *bitmapping*), an outline font can be scaled, or resized, to any size without getting jaggy edges. Both *TrueType* and *PostScript* fonts are outline fonts. See those chapters.

output

Output refers to what is put out of your computer. It may refer to *hard copy,* the output that comes from your printer. It may refer to the screen display, which is output to your eyes.

pair kerning

Pair kerning refers to the pairs of *kerned* characters that a designer has built into a font. What!? Well, when a font is designed, every character is created with a certain amount of space following it so letters don't bump into each other. But there are always certain pairs of characters that do not fit well together, such as **To** or **Va,** because of the space within their shapes. So a designer usually finds the worst 300 or 400 pairs and creates a kerning pair for each combination, a little unit that has a special spacing arrangement. These kerning pairs are part of the font.

Most word processors are not sophisticated enough to take advantage of the kerning pairs. In page layout applications like PageMaker or QuarkXPress, however, you can choose to have the kerning pairs appear automatically as you type, or you can be more specific and choose to have them appear only if you use type above a specified size. Typically, kerning pairs are really only needed in type sizes over 11 or 12 point.

PE   On *galleys* of typeset type or on laser printed copy, you may see the initials **PE,** which stand for Printer's Error. This notation means the error was the fault of the person who was typesetting the page or laying it out or printing it and the correction should not be charged to the client. See AA (author's alterations).

pen advance   The **pen advance** is the amount of space after a character. It is the amount you would have advanced your pen before you wrote the next character. The pen advance is designed into a typeface.

pi font   A **pi font** is a font that uses specialized characters, such as those for science, math, cartography, etc., instead of our standard alphanumeric characters.

pica (1)   A **pica** is the basic unit of measure typesetters have used for the past 100 years to specify type sizes, line lengths, and the space between lines (the *leading*). There are 6 picas in 1 inch; each pica is divided into 12 *points.* Thus there are 72 points per inch.

Actually, type size and *leading* is measured in *points,* and horizontal measurements, such as line length, are usually measured in picas. For instance, you might create a brochure with 10-point type, 12-point leading, and columns 24 picas wide (written as 10/12 x 24, pronounced 10 on 12 by 24).

For purists who know that traditionally 72 points does not equal exactly one inch, but only .996 of an inch, you will be interested to learn that on the Macintosh 72 points really does equal exactly one inch. The original Macintosh screen was 72 pixels per inch (that was not an accident).

pica (2)   **Pica** is also the term for a certain kind of generic type that has 10 characters per inch, as opposed to *elite* type that has 12 characters per inch. The terms "pica" and "elite" are not actually referring to a particular typeface, but to the *pitch,* which is the number of characters in a given measurement. Both pica and elite typefaces are *monospaced.*

picture font   A **picture font** is a font that has little pictures instead of characters. They are useful for making quick logos, interesting bullets, or decorative borders. Each of the pictures below is actually a character in a font.

point   A **point** is $^1/_{72}$ of an inch. There are 12 points in one *pica*. There are 72 points in one inch. Points are used to measure type size (the type you are reading is 9 point) and the space between lines and paragraphs. Points are used to measure the thickness of *rules,* or drawn lines. Please also see *pica.*

PostScript

PostScript is a very powerful graphical computer language that can tell a printer how to create complex letterforms and graphics. PostScript is a "page description language," meaning it talks to the printer, not to the computer (the Macintosh screen understands the language *QuickDraw*). Not all printers can interpret PostScript, though (see *PostScript printer,* below).

PostScript printer

A **PostScript printer** has its own cPU (central processing unit), its own RAM (memory), and its own ROM (read-only memory). This is what makes a Post-Script printer so expensive—it's actually another form of computer. This printer can read the "page description language" called *PostScript.* Please see Chapter I for details on the PostScript language and printers.

PostScript-compatible printer

A **PostScript-compatible printer** is a printer that doesn't *really* understand *PostScript,* but it can fake it pretty well. Some people feel if you're going to be doing heavy graphics and professional-level typesetting, you should spend the few extra bucks on a true PostScript printer. Others claim PostScript compatible printers are incredible workhorses for all levels of jobs.

prime mark

A **prime mark** is the technical term for the character we use as a foot mark ('). Notice it is not really the typewriter apostrophe (') because a prime mark is at a slant. The double prime is the correct symbol for inch ("). The symbols you see here are printed from the Symbol font (Option 4 for the ', Option Comma for the "). If you don't have the Symbol font, you can italicize the single and double typewriter quote marks (' "). If you use these characters regularly, or even if you use them a lot in just one document, take advantage of the search-and-replace feature in your application to make it easier.

printer font

A **printer font,** sometimes called an *outline font,* is actually a mathematical formula that tells a printer how to create a particular typeface. Because of this mathematical outline (rather than simple *bitmapping*), an outline font can be scaled, or resized, to any size without getting jaggy edges. Both *TrueType* and *PostScript* fonts are outline fonts. See those chapters.

proof

A **proof** is the final printed draft. If the proof is perfect, then you can proceed to printing your final version, ready for reproduction.

proportional spacing

Proportional spacing means that the letters on the page each take up a relative, or proportional, amount of space according to how wide they are. For instance, the letter "W" takes up significantly more room than the letter "i" or a period. Now, you may think this is only logical. But on the typewriter that many of us grew up on, proportional spacing was just about non-existent—typewriters use *monospacing:* on a typewriter and on some primitive computer screens, the letter "i" takes up as much space as the letter "w." If you drew vertical lines between the letters of a monospaced paragraph, all the letters would line up in columns (see the example under *monospacing*). Most computers at this point in history are capable of producing text with proportional spacing, which looks much more professional and is much more *readable.* What you are reading right now is proportionally spaced type.

punctuation

Punctuation refers to all the characters in a font that are used to define our grammar, such as commas, question marks, periods, exclamation points, semicolons, colons, etc. All these characters are included in a *character set,* along with all *capitals, lowercase* letters, and other necessary symbols.

quad left, right

Quad left or **quad right** are the same as *flush left* or *flush right.* It means the text is lined up on the left or the right side of the column. Unless specified otherwise, the opposite side is *ragged,* or not lined up.

QuickDraw

QuickDraw is the graphical description language the Macintosh uses to draw the text and the graphics on your screen. It is not the language a *PostScript printer* reads, though.

QuickDraw printer

A **QuickDraw printer** is a printer that is capable only of reproducing what it finds on the computer screen. If your type or graphics look chunky and ugly on the screen, they will look chunky and ugly when printed on a QuickDraw printer. If you use *Adobe Type Manager* with *PostScript* fonts or if you use *TrueType,* then your type (but not necessarily your graphics) will be as smooth and lovely as can be. A QuickDraw printer cannot interpret *PostScript.*

quotation mark

These are **quotation marks:** " ". This is not a quotation mark: ". Quotation marks curl in toward the text, so there is an opening quote and a closing quote. They are sometimes called "sixes and nines" as a mnemonic for remembering which way the curl goes.

Qwerty

The **Qwerty keyboard** is the one you probably have. It's the standard sort of keyboard whose first six characters are the letters q, w, e, r, t, and y. The arrangement of the keys was intentionally designed to slow down speedy typists so the machine wouldn't jam. Compare with *Dvorak keyboard.*

rag, ragged

If your type is not *justified,* then the edge that is not aligned is called **ragged.** Ideally you want to try to keep the ragged edge as smooth as possible. If there are one or two lines that hang out much longer or a line that is significantly shorter, they call too much attention to themselves and disrupt the aesthetics. If someone tells you to "fix the **rag**," it means the ragged edge of your type is *too* ragged.

ragged left

Ragged left type is type that is aligned on the right edge and unaligned (ragged) on the left. Also see *alignment.*

ragged right

Ragged right type is type that is aligned on the left edge and unaligned (ragged) on the right. It is the easiest sort of text alignment to read. Also see *alignment.*

range kerning

Range kerning refers to adjusting the letter spacing over a range (group) of characters, as opposed to *manual kerning* which is adjusting the space between two characters. See *kerning.*

raster

Raster means to turn something into dots that can be printed or that can be displayed on your computer screen (two different forms of *output*). *Object-oriented* images and *PostScript* images are created with a series of math formulas and straight lines. But neither the computer screen nor any printer can print these straight, object-oriented lines. They can only output tiny dots.

So you might draw what looks to you like a circle, and the computer understands it to be an object with a mathematical formula holding thousands of little straight lines together, but that image goes through a rasterizing process that turns the formula into electronic bits of information that light up certain dots on your screen.

When you print to your *PostScript printer,* the computer inside the printer rasterizes the images and the text.

When you print to an *imagesetter,* there is a special piece of hardware whose job is to rasterize the page (called a RIP, raster image processor).

When you print to a *QuickDraw printer,* the Mac sends the bitmapped data down to the printer.

Since the rasterizing process is basically creating bitmapped information, some people simplify the whole thing and say that a raster is a just another word for a displayed bitmap.

TrueType fonts include the technology to rasterize the characters to the screen and to any printer, which is why TrueType fonts look smooth around the edges. If you use PostScript fonts, then you can use *Adobe Type Manager* to rasterize your fonts, both to the screen and to any printer.

readability

Readability is different from *legibility.* Readability refers to how easy it is to read an extensive amount of text. It depends on the design of the typeface, on how long the lines of text are, how much space is between the lines, the style (bold, italic, etc.) of the type, and other factors. The most readable typefaces are those that are "invisible"; that is, they have no distinguishing features that make your eye trip. *Serif* typefaces (like this one you are reading right now) are generally more readable than *sans serif* typefaces.

recto

Recto is the right-hand page in a book. Rectos are always odd-numbered pages. Left-hand pages are called *verso.*

resident font

A **resident font** is a font that lives in your printer. Resident fonts are sometimes known as "built-in fonts." The *LaserWriter 35* are resident in the Apple LaserWriters. Please see Chapter 5 on PostScript fonts.

resolution (printer)

Resolution on the printer refers to how many *dots per inch* are created in the *output;* that is, how many rows of horizontal dots are in an inch on the printed paper. For instance, on a typical laser printer, the images are built out of 600 dots per inch. On an *imagesetter,* the resolution can be from 1,270 to 2,540 dots per inch. Obviously, the higher the resolution, the smoother and sharper the text or image.

resolution (monitor) **Resolution** on a monitor is not defined by the number of dots or pixels (dots on the screen) per inch, as in the definition for printer resolution, above, since most monitors have around 72 pixels per inch. Screen resolution, or how well an image is "resolved," is determined by the range of grays or colors that each pixel can display. The greater the range of colors, the easier it is to create a smoother-appearing image. The range of each pixel is determined by the bit depth. If you really want details and illustrations on monitor resolution, please see the lengthy description in my book, *The Non-Designer's Web Book.*

reverse **Reverse** text is text that is white on a black background. Actually, it is any white text that is on a dark background. If you are going to reverse text, make it a point size or two larger than usual, and make it a little bolder than usual. If possible, avoid reversing type smaller than about 20 points, or type that has delicate features like thin serifs or sharp points.

Small type with thin hairlines is inappropriate for reverse text.

Use bolder, larger type when you want to reverse it.

river When you try to *justify* type (align it on both sides of the column) on a line length that is too short for the size of the font, the computer has to force extra space between some words to make the text reach out to the edges. When there are several of these wide word spaces near each other in a paragraph, it creates what appears to be a **river** of white space flowing through the text. Turn your text upside down, angle it slightly away from you, and squint at it. You will be able to see any rivers clearly. Avoid creating rivers. Sometimes it means you have to rewrite copy, or adjust the margins of the page, adjust the point size of the text slightly, or use a variety of other techniques depending on the capabilities of your software. Usually just removing the justification will eliminate the rivers.

"Hoe-cake, murder," re-splendent Ladle Rat Rotten Hut, an tickle ladle basking an stuttered oft. Honor wrote tutor cordage offer groin murder, Ladle Rat Rotten Hut mitten anomalous woof.

Can you see the wide river flowing through this text?

roman **Roman** applies to any typeface, *serif* or *sans serif,* that is not slanted. If it is not *italic,* then it is roman. Often, on the Mac, a typeface is called a roman when it is not bold or extended or any other variety—when it is just the plain vanilla flavor of the font.

rule

A **rule** is typesetter jargon for a drawn line. This is a rule: ——————

run-around

Run-around refers to text that flows around a graphic or some other sort of shape, maybe even a blank space. It's also called a "wrap around," "text wrap," or "contour type." The text below runs around the graphic that is placed between the columns.

"Wail, wail, wail!" set disk wicket woof, "Evanescent Ladle Rat Rotten Hut! Wares are putty ladle gull goring wizard ladle basking?"

"Armor goring tumor groin-murder's," reprisal ladle gull. "Grammar's seeking bet. Armor ticking arson burden barter an shirker cockles."

"O hoe! Heifer gnats woke," setter wicket woof, butter taught tomb shelf, "Oil tickle shirt court. Oil ketchup wetter letter, an den—O bore!"

Soda wicket woof tucker shirt court, an whinney retched a cordage offer groin-murder, picked inner windrow, an sore debtor pore oil worming

running head

A **running head** is a line of type that occurs regularly in a multi-page publication, usually at the top of the page. This book has running heads at the top of each page. Sometimes the running head tells you what book you are reading (in case you have forgotten), the author's name (in case you want to be reminded on every page), the chapter title, the first or last dictionary entry, or other pertinent information.

sans serif

Sans serif is a category of type with letterforms that have no *serifs* (since "sans" is French for "without"). Sans serif typefaces tend to have no *thick-thin* transition in their letterforms; that is, the strokes are usually monoweight (the same thickness all the way around the letter). Also see *serif.*

Serif **Sans Serif**

scalable font

A **scalable font** is a font that can be resized on the screen to any point size without becoming distorted or jaggy-edged because of the limited resolution. Both *TrueType* and *PostScript* are scalable font formats. They are also called *outline fonts.* Please see Chapter 5 for more details.

screen font

A **screen font** is the *bitmapped* portion of a typeface that is used to display the type on the screen. Even if you are using *ATM (Adobe Type Manager),* which builds the on-screen type using the *outline* or *printer font,* you still need the screen font installed so the font name will appear in your menu. Please see Part I of this book for a comparision of all these font terms.

script

Script refers to a category of type that emulates handwriting. This category can be further broken down into scripts that connect, scripts that are casual, fancy, hand printed, etc.

This script face is called Shelley Volante.

serif

A **serif** is the tiny stroke at the ends of the major strokes of a letterform. Serifs comes in a wide variety, from very thin to very thick, horizontal or slanted, *bracketed* or unbracketed, rounded or truncated, etc. A typeface that has serifs on its characters is considered a "serif typeface." Also see *sans serif.*

These are serifs.

service bureau

A **service bureau** is a business where you can take your disk with your publication on it and have the publication printed on an *imagesetter* with a much higher *resolution* than you have on your personal printer at home. If you have a laser printer or a DeskJet, DeskWriter, StyleWriter, or some other similar sort of printer, your resolution is around 300 to 600 dots per inch. An imagesetter prints your document onto resin-coated photo paper (smooth and thicker) with a resolution from 1,270 to 2,540 dots per inch.

Service bureaus can output (print out) your document onto transparent film, if necessary, or sometimes to a color printer or to slides. Some service bureaus offer the service of scanning photographs or artwork for you, or letting you use their laser printer (for a fee, of course). A rare service bureau even has self-service imagesetting.

set width

The **set width** of a character is the specific horizontal width that is built into a character when it is designed. It originally referred to the space before and after the character itself, also. Some programs let you change the set width, let you *expand* or *condense* the letterforms. Please don't do this arbitrarily— the computer doesn't redesign the font, it just squishes or stretches the text (see the example under *true-drawn*).

sfnt

The **sfnt** is a font identification structure for *TrueType* fonts, similar to NFNT for *PostScript* fonts.

slab serif

Slab serif is a category of type that includes those faces with chunky, slab-like *serifs.* Slab serif type is often "monoweight" or almost monoweight, meaning there is little or no *thick-to-thin* transition in the main strokes of the letters, as you can see in the light and bold weights below.

This is a **slab serif.** *Notice the horizontal slabs for serifs.*

small caps

SMALL CAPS IS A STYLE VARIATION (LIKE THIS) where instead of having capital letters in the regular size, the caps are about the size of the lowercase letters. Unfortunately, on the computer the stylistic change to small caps just reduces the size of the regular capital letter. This means the stroke width and proportions are smaller also, making the first regular capital appear significantly and disproportionately heavier than the small caps. The solution is to invest in an *expert set,* most of which include a special font for small caps that have been redesigned to match the weight and proportions of the regular capital (see *true-drawn*).

smart apostrophe

A **smart apostrophe** refers to a real apostrophe—not a fake one, a straight one, a dumb one, a typewriter apostrophe. This is a smart apostrophe: ' . This is not a smart apostrophe: ' .

smart quote

A **smart quote** refers to a real quotation mark—not a fake one, a straight one, a dumb one, a typewriter quote. These are smart quotes: " " . These are not smart quotes: " " . Notice the real quotation marks turn in toward the sentence; there is an "opening" quote mark and a "closing" quote mark. Single quotes also have an opening and a closing curve to them.

The term "smart quote" is actually from a tiny software utility that automatically substituted true opening and closing single and double quotation marks when you typed the typewriter marks.

solid

If text is set **solid,** it means there is no extra *leading* (space) between the lines of type. This does not necessarily mean the two lines of type will bump into each other because there is usually some *body clearance* built into a typeface.

spaceband

A **spaceband** is the technical term for the space created by the Spacebar. The spaceband is created by the designer along with all the characters.

stet

Stet, usually handwritten in the margin or between the lines, means to ignore the change that was previously marked on the page, to leave it the way it was. Stet is Latin for "let it stand."

stress

Most letterforms have a *thick-to-thin* transition in the strokes, particularly obvious in the curved strokes. If you look at a capital letter "O" and draw a line through the thinnest parts of the letter, that would show you the **stress** of the typeface. A face might have a diagonal stress or perhaps a vertical stress. Typefaces with *monoweight* strokes have no stress at all.

stroke

In a character, a **stroke** is a single straight or curved line.

suitcase

Futile

This is a typical suitcase icon in which you can store bitmapped fonts.

A **suitcase** is the kind of computer file that *screen fonts* are stored within. It is so-called because the icon looks like a little suitcase. In Mac OS 8 and any version of System 7, each size of *bitmapped screen font* has its own file and icon, and can be stored in suitcase files or loose in any folder.

Confusion arises with these suitcases because a popular font management utility is called Suitcase and people think there must be a connection or maybe they are the same thing. There isn't, really, and they're not, except that the Suitcase *utility* takes advantage of the suitcase *icons* for organizing fonts.

Suitcase™

Suitcase is a *utility* or small application that helps you manage your fonts. It is different from and has almost nothing to do with the suitcase icons. Please see Chapter 12 on Suitcase in the font management section.

swash
Swash is the term for those characters that have a fancy little curlicue on some part of the letter. Many swashes look dumb because they are just stuck on the end of an existing letter rather than designed into the entire letterform. Be careful about using swash characters; it's easy to overdo them. Swashes are generally meant to be placed at the beginning or the end of a phrase, not in the middle unless the swash does not interrupt the letterspacing of the rest of the paragraph.

text
Text is the information that is to be typeset or even that has already been typeset and is on your screen, waiting for you to edit and *format.* We use the word "text" to differentiate from "graphics." The text is referred to as the *copy.*

thick-thin
In the stroke of a letterform, the term **thick-thin** refers to whether there is a transition in the stroke from a thick portion to a thin portion. Different categories of type tend to have either a moderate thick-thin transition, as in *oldstyle,* or a radical thick-thin transition, as in *modern. Sans serifs* and *slab serifs* have little or no transition in the strokes.

Notice how the strokes of these "o"s alternate (or don't) between thick and thin.

O   o   O   O

thin space
A **thin space** is an empty space character that is one-fourth the width of an *em.* An em is a space that is the width of the point size of the type, so if the type is 12 points, then the width of a thin space is 3 points. In most software programs, these em, en, and thin spaces are *hard, non-breaking spaces.*

tracking
Tracking is an adjustment of the letter spacing. True tracking is **point-size dependent,** meaning the amount of letterspacing that is adjusted depends on the point size of the type (larger type needs less space between the letters, and smaller type needs more space). Selecting a group of characters and removing a set amount of space between them is *not* tracking—that is *range kerning.* A discussion of manual kerning, range kerning, tracking, pair kerning, auto kerning, etc., is in my book, *The Non-Designer's Type Book.*

transitional
Transitional is a typeface category with only a few faces in it, Baskerville being the classic. It is a category that falls between *oldstyle* and *modern,* where the letterforms were becoming more mechanically drawn, having a stronger *thick-thin* contrast than the oldstyles and with less *stress.*

true-drawn
True-drawn refers to typefaces that have been drawn by the designer rather than modified by the computer. For instance, it is possible to condense a typeface right on the screen—the computer just squishes it. But if a designer

originally created the font as a condensed face, she redesigned the proportions, the counters, the x-height to cap-height ratio, the thick-thin transitions, etc. Here is an example of a computer-generated condensed face and a true-drawn condensed face:

Franklin Gothic, Computer Squished

Franklin Gothic Extra Condensed, True-Drawn

Small caps can also be created right on the screen by the computer, but it is preferable to use true-drawn small caps, such as those that are included in *expert set* fonts. In the examples below, notice the stroke width in the capital letters as opposed to the small caps; in the true-drawn letters, the strokes of the small caps match proportionally with the regular caps.

SMALL CAPS FAKING IT   TRUE-DRAWN SMALL CAPS

TrueType	**TrueType** is Apple's font technology. TrueType fonts can look smooth at any size on the screen, rather than looking jagged when in any size that is not *installed*. TrueType is sometimes best for people who do not have *PostScript printers*. Please see Chapter 8 on TrueType.
Type 1 font	A **Type 1 font** is a *PostScript outline font*. This means it is created in such a way that a *PostScript printer* can interpret its form and will print it clean and smooth at any size on a PostScript printer. Type 1 fonts are specially designed to be able to print clearly at small sizes on low-resolution machines (low resolution here meaning 300 *dots per inch*). Several years ago only the Adobe Corporation could create Type 1 fonts; now all vendors can create them. Please see Chapter 5 on PostScript for details of Type 1 and Type 3 fonts.
Type 2 font	There is no such thing as a **Type 2** font. It was a technology from Adobe that was never actually released.
Type 3 font	**Type 3 font** technology is what everyone else had to use while Adobe had the secrets to *Type 1* and wouldn't tell; only Adobe could create Type 1 fonts and everyone else had to create Type 3 fonts. Please see Chapter 5 on PostScript for details of Type 1 and Type 3 fonts.
typeface	A **typeface** is specific, named design of type. Please see *font* and the difference between a font and a typeface; page 15.
typeset, typesetting	**Typesetting** is the process of turning typewritten or handwritten information into **typeset,** or professionally prepared, type, ready to be reproduced.
type size	The **type size** (the height of type) is measured in *points*. There are 72 points in one inch. What you read in a book is usually about 9 to 11 point type; newsletter headlines are typically around 18 to 24 point type.
type style	**Type style** can refer to the same thing as a *typeface*, but it usually refers to a particular characteristic of a typeface, such as *italic* or *bold* or *reverse*.

typo	**Typo** is short for "typographical error," those embarrassing mistakes you make while typing, mistakes like stupid misspellings or transposing characters. Isn't it amazing how many typos you never see until the job is comlpeted?
typography	**Typography** is the art or process of creating with type and letterforms. It also refers to the general character or appearance of printed matter. You can say, "She's not a great designer, but her typography is always dynamic."
U/lc, U&lc	**U/lc** stands for *upper* and *lowercase*. You might also see it as C/lc for Caps, lower case. Written as **U&lc** (pronounced "you en el see"), it is the name of a particularly wonderful tabloid from ITC (International Typeface Corporation).
UC, Uc, U.C.	**UC** (or any variation) stands for **u**pper**c**ase.
underline	An **underline** is something you should never use in professional-level type. An underline is a proofreader's mark indicating that the underlined text is really supposed to be *italic* (or if all the text is already italic, the underlined words should be *roman*). On a typewriter, we had to underline text because we had no italic. On the computer, the underline sits too close to the text; often it hangs right on the *baseline* and disturbs the characters. There are several alternatives to using an underline.

Don't type underlines, please. *Use italic* or **bold** or **another face.**

underscore	**Underscore** is the same as *underline*.
unjustified	**Unjustified** means the type does not line up straight on both the left and the right sides. It may be lined up on the left and *ragged* on the right, or vice versa, or it may be centered or it may be completely asymmetrical. This paragraph is set unjustified.
uppercase	*Capital* letters are also known as **uppercase** letters. You can use the word as a noun, as in "UPPERCASE IS MORE DIFFICULT TO READ," or as an adjective, as in "Please don't type my name in all uppercase letters."
	The word "uppercase" is from the days when all type was created with metal letters. The tiny pieces of metal type were kept in large, flat cases with a separate cubby for each letter. There was a case for the capital letters and a separate case for the small letters. In the racks that held the cases, the case for the capital letters was above the case for the small letters. Thus the capitals became known as "uppercase" and the small letters as "lowercase." The California job case, designed in the 1800s, held all the letters, caps and small, in one flat case.
utility	A **utility** is a little software program that isn't really meant for you to create anything in, and it doesn't let you make anything to print, it just helps you get your work done. Many utilities work with no help from you at all.
verso	**Verso** refers to the left-hand page of a book. Versos are ***always*** even-numbered. The right-hand page of a book is the *recto,* and yes, the recto is always odd-numbered.

vertical justification **Vertical justification** refers to aligning the tops and bottoms of columns to some point, either to each other if they are adjacent, or perhaps just to fill a defined space. For instance, if you have a column that is 23.5 picas deep and you really need it to be 24 picas deep, you need to vertically justify the column. One way to do this is by feathering in a tiny bit of extra linespace (leading); if your leading in the column is currently 13 points, try changing it to 13.3 to fill the space. Some programs can vertically justify a column automatically.

virgule **Virgule** (pronounced "ver gyool") is a generic term for a slash: /. The regular slash is different from the *fraction bar.*

weight The **weight** of a typeface refers to the thickness of the strokes that form the letter. The thicker the stroke, the "heavier" the typeface.
This typeface is a light weight.   **This typeface is a heavy weight.**

widow There is great debate over the exact definition of a **widow.** I define a widow as a very short last line of a paragraph, a line that is too short in relation to the width of the paragraph. I usually tell beginners to never leave less than seven characters on a line by themselves, but really the actual number is visual— if it looks too short, it *is* too short. In a wide paragraph, twelve characters may be too short. In a narrow paragraph, six characters may be sufficient. It doesn't matter what you call it or how many letters you define it as, the point is not to do it. Widows are an aesthetically disturbing sight. The worst kind of widow is a hyphenated word that leaves the last part of the last word hanging.

word spacing **Word spacing** refers to the space between the words. When designing a font, the designer also determines the amount of space that will be between words. Sometimes you may need to adjust that space, depending on the font and what you are creating with it.

x-height The **x-height** is the height of the lowercase letter "x." That letter has been chosen as a standard from which to judge the visual size of letters because it is the only character that has all four corners touching the outer boundaries— there's no question as to the top or bottom or sides of an **x** as there might be for the letter **c.**

It is the x-height of a font that determines how large the font appears to be. The relative x-height to "cap height" (height of the capital letters) is one of the determining factors in the legibility and the readability of a typeface.

This is the 30-point size of the entire body. hop hop *hop* **hop**

These examples are all 30-point type. The impression that one is larger than another comes mainly from the x-height. Within the 30-point body of the typeface, the designer can fill the space however she feels like it.

Part VI
Index

Other books you may need

by Robin Williams

The Non-Designer's Design Book
*Design and typographic principles for the
visual novice. Beginners and professionals
alike seem to love this book. It works.*

The Non-Designer's Type Book
*More sophisticated typographic insights and
secrets (previously titled* Beyond the Mac is
not a typewriter*). One of my favorite books.*

The Non-Designer's Web Book
*An easy guide to creating, designing, and
posting your own web site, from start to
finish; this book gets rave reviews from
designers and non-designers alike.
Written with John Tollett.*

A Blip in the Continuum
*A celebration of ugly typography! Illustrated
by John Tollett. Just plain ol' darn fun.*

The Mac is not a typewriter
*A style manual for creating professional-
level type on your Macintosh; the basics
you absolutely must know.*

The Little Mac Book
*The best-selling, award-winning, beginner's
guide to using the Macintosh.*

Beyond The Little Mac Book
This book takes up where The Little Mac
Book *leaves off; written with Steve Broback.*

All books are available at your local
bookstore, through Peachpit Press,
or any online bookstore.

Peachpit Press
1249 Eighth Street
Berkeley, California 94710
510.524.2178 phone
510.524.2221 fax
www.peachpit.com

colophon

About this book

I created this book in PageMaker 6.5, the best tool for book publishing. The index and the table of contents were generated right within PageMaker. It's too cool.

The body text font is the Linotype Centennial family with the expert set collection, originally from Linotype-Hell. This face has a very large x-height, so the body text type size is 9.6 with 13-point leading. The heads are Formata Bold, from Adobe Systems. The section titles are Shelley Volante from Adobe.

About this author

I live in New Mexico on 2.5 acres of beautiful high desert country. I see the dramatic sunrise every morning and the sunset every evening. I have three great kids who are growing up, and four dogs. I teach electronic typography at Santa Fe Community College, and I'm a founder and am active in the Santa Fe Mac Users Group, the New Mexico Internet Professionals Association, and the Wild Web Women of Santa Fe. I travel anywhere someone asks me to and give workshops and seminars on a variety of topics. I am having a grand adventure.

Robin